T0149858

Saving Black America:
An Economic Plan for Civil Rights

by

John Yancy Odom, Ph.D.

At the bottom of education,
At the bottom of politics,
Even at the bottom of religion,
There must be for our race
Economic independence.

—Booker T. Washington

Front Cover illustration by Angelo Williams
The second photo on cover is Charles Hamilton, a major champion of
the civil rights movement.
Copyright © 2001 by John Yancy Odom, Ph.D.
First Edition, First Printing

Chicago, Illinois

Printed in the United States of America

ISBN: 0-913543-73-X

Saving Black America:
An Economic Plan for Civil Rights

CONTENTS

To Nikki, Dionte, Shantel, Chaniqua and all Black children — here is more hope.

> The only way that we as Black people are going to get anything is through ownership, because ownership brings power...We don't have enough power. That's why we can't change things...The banks are the ones we should really be talking to, not the government.
>
> - Ervin "Magic" Johnson
> (after the 1992 Los Angeles riot)

> Let none hear you idly saying, There is nothing
> I can do;
> While the souls of men are dying, And the Master
> calls for you.
>
> Take the task He gives you gladly, Let His work
> your pleasure be;
> Answer quickly when He calleth, "Here am I,
> send me, send me."
>
> Daniel March
> J. C. Lenderman

ACKNOWLEDGMENTS

The end of this publication odyssey has caused me to think about a number of people who walked with me for stretches, were present at critical junctures or who crossed my path at important times. Most contributed encouragement, but some may not remember why his or her name is being mentioned. I do remember and am nonetheless grateful for them. So, I mention them with appreciation. They are as follows: Ben Odom, Luther Odom, Judson Odom, Corey Odom, Dr. Jawanza Kunjufu, George Fraser, Kwame Salter, Norm D'Amours, Eric Postel, Dan Neviaser, Paul Soglin, Pete Crear, Steve Morrison, Attys. Allan Koritzinsky and G. F. Monday of Foley & Lardner, Sybil Evans, The National Professionals Network, J. B. Guinn, Dr. Alvin McLean, Dr. Booker Gardner, Ron LaMascus, Trudy Barash, Elder Eugene Johnson, Dolores Greene, Marie Brown, Debra Macewiscz, LaDonna Radel, Arline Hess and Donna Williams.

In the spirit of the last being first, I thank dear Ann and the Holy Trinity.

FOREWORD

John Odom is onto something. Something significant. But before I expound on what that something is, I want to tell how John and I came to know each other, because I believe that people share time and space for a reason.

In August of 2000, I was a keynote speaker for a conference at sea. My address was an extension of my life's mission — to promote the advancement of the African Diaspora through economic development and economic development through networking.

On the cruise, I addressed the conference as a member of a powerful panel, which included Kweisi Mfume, Les Brown and Bishop T. D. Jakes. The comments I made represent my core beliefs — that Black people are not poor! We are, in truth, wealthy. We are a 572 billion dollar annual economy, and if we were a nation, we would be the 11th richest in the world. Over the last 35 years, Black baby boomers alone have passed over 500 billion hours of formal education and professional training, worth in excess of 5 trillion dollars.

Nearly 60 percent of our workforces — 9 million of us, are in executive, managerial, supervisory, professional, specialty, technical, vocational administrative sales and business ownership positions. That is an army of potential role models and mentors to help those who are less fortunate or stuck in cycles of poverty. In fact, there is no army larger than the army of Black folks who have succeeded in this country.

If the truth were known, we are the "beacon of hope" for every single person of African descent in the entire world. So make no mistake, success runs in our race.

And because we are the only culture in the history of mankind that, because of slavery, had to put political empowerment before economic empowerment, we have successfully elected over 9,000 public officials. Nonetheless, we are still at the bottom of the educational and economic heap, primarily because we have asked our elected officials and our ministers to be responsible for improving every aspect of our lives.

It is my belief that, unfortunately, Black folk operate on 100 year cycles. For example, our 100 year fight (1864-1964) for civil rights, voting rights and public access was a unifying purpose and anyone Black in America could identify with it. To that end, it seems to me, Black America has identified economic development, closing the income and wealth gap, as our next unifying purpose.

In staging ourselves to act on our unifying purpose, we have surpassed W.E.B. DuBois' dream of the talented 10th. Today, nearly 14 percent of African Americans have at least a 4-year college degree. We have a lot of PhD's, no we need some Ph.DO's to bring economic development into the fore as a civil rights strategy. Enter John Y. Odom, Ph.D.

Saving Black America: An Economic Plan for Civil Rights is a major contribution to the next and long overdue phase in the progression of civil rights for African Americans — that of interconnecting resources for economic empowerment and wealth building. Through adroit reasoning, common sense and bold proposals, Dr. Odom has analyzed and memorialized that which many forward thinking brothers and sisters have been saying for decades — it's economics this time! And that is the mark of a true contribution — to cause thinking people to say, "Why didn't I think of that?!" or "I thought of that, but I didn't write it down!" John has thought of it and he has written it down.

His easy writing style and clear examples aside, the nub of *Saving Black America* is that nothing good happens without a structure to assure that good happens. That the creation, maintenance and improvement of a sound organizational structure is the primary work of people who plan for success, be it in business, education, religion, social services or civil rights. Particularly useful are the chapters on the Quebec credit union system and Jewish federations as examples that others have done what John proposes for Black Americans.

By training and experience, John is an educator and consultant. At heart, though, John is a divergent thinker and a fellow civil rights warrior who has dedicated his life to making a difference for our people.

From a distance it may appear that my strategy of intentional and intensive networking and John's strategy of a loose hierarchy to achieve economic civil rights are at odds. Nothing could be further from the truth. There can be more than one right answer, and with the Herculean task ahead of Black America, all good strategies should be tried simultaneously. The overlaying of a hierarchy on a network creates a grid that insures greater success.

As a result, I highly recommend this book to all people who are interested in the advancement of our race. I have pledged to John my unqualified support for his efforts, because I am confident that this work and the works that build on it will represent a leap forward for the cause of Black people.

One writer has said that the first requirement of intelligent tinkering is to save all the pieces. *Saving Black America* represents a big puzzle piece.

John Odom is onto something significant that will help advance the cause of economic empowerment as a civil rights strategy.

George C. Fraser, Author
Race for Success and *Success Runs in Our Race*
Publisher, *Success Guide Millennium 2000-2001*

INTRODUCTION
Why and How

Why

"Nothing ever built arose to touch the skies unless some man dreamed that it should, some man believed that it could, and some man willed that it must."
— Charles Franklin Kettering

Saving Black America is about transforming the civil rights movement to respond effectively to the current challenges facing Black America. My experiences as a Black American, my roots in the southern Black experience of the '50's and '60's, my educational experiences and an active professional life convince me that a new direction for civil rights is essential and woefully overdue.

In this book I will unveil a basis for transforming the civil rights movement. Aspects of this background will sound familiar to forward thinking Black readers. To them, I seek your indulgence as I interpret our shared condition through my experiential lens. Later, I will share ideas unique to me. To readers not steeped in the Black experience or in the genre of civil rights transformation, many insights may be revelatory. I invite those readers to contemplate and act.

I will discuss the importance of contemplation as a precondition to change — to take stock and to receive inspiration in order to avoid falling into the comfort of old patterns or becoming overwhelmed or acting precipitously.

This book is a natural extension of my life, which has been heavily influenced by civil rights and, as a result, change. Consequently, institutional change is a topic of significant interest to me both professionally and as a volunteer. I bring to the civil rights movement both dedication and skepticism.

My interest in civil rights and change were indelibly imprinted by my upbringing. I was born in 1948 in Jackson, Mississippi. Because my father was a minister in the Christian Methodist Episcopal Church (C.M.E.), after a time, he would move to a church in a different city. As a result, my formative years were enriched and influenced by periods in Jackson, Mississippi, Little Rock, Arkansas (I was in elementary school during the historic integration of Central High School), and

Jackson, Tennessee. I was educated in segregated public schools and I earned my bachelor's degree from C.M.E. affiliated Lane College, a historically Black college in Jackson, Tennessee.

My father, the late Rev. C. F. Odom (Reverend) was, as one of his contemporaries called him, "a Christian gentleman" and a no-nonsense civil rights advocate from the 1930's until his passing in 1979. Reverend did not discriminate. Foolishness was foolishness, White or Black, he was against foolishness.

Taking cues as a youth, I was busy in: the church, academic pursuits, music, acting, leadership positions and in civil rights. And amid many similar interests as an adult, civil rights remain a backdrop for my life.

The child is truly father of the man. As a teacher, my motivation was multicultural education. My first administrative post was as an Affirmative Action officer, my second was that of Director of Human Relations, and my 1977 doctoral thesis at the University of Wisconsin-Madison was on Human Relations in the field of Educational Administration. As a consultant, the topics of Workforce Diversity and intergroup relations are specialties, and as a volunteer, I have worked with many organizations to improve civil rights, including as President of the Madison, Wisconsin Branch of the NAACP and on the NAACP's National Strategic Task Force on Education.

My life experiences would never permit me to ignore civil rights, yet the civil rights movement, like all movements, has its own inertia that compels individuals to float in its stream. Nonetheless, there comes a time to swim against the current, to struggle upstream in order to redirect the flow to achieve the time-honored goals of justice, equality and fairness more efficiently and effectively. *Saving Black America* is my report on why and how to swim up the civil rights stream.

Recently, *Parade*[1] magazine featured a story about Randi Altschul who, at age 40, was granted her 2,000th U. S. patent. Altschul, a college drop-out, has been registering patents since she was 12. Altschul says, "My greatest asset is that I don't know anything. I have no proper training in engineering or art or anything. That means I have no boundaries."

This article reminded me of a discussion I had with a book agent a while ago. "Who are you to write a book on a new direction for civil rights?" she asked. "Like it or not, a person has to be well-known in an area before publishers will consider the manuscript." This was a discouraging revelation. At 50 years old, I had flashes of a life wasted and an urge to organize a March on Washington!

Then, I recalled the words of futurist Joel Barker[2] who defines a paradigm as a set of rules and regulations that establishes boundaries and dictates to individuals the behaviors required for success within those boundaries. He *suggested that honors await* those who use the current paradigm, the status quo, to solve unsolved problems.

Barker defined a paradigm shift as a new game with a new set of rules. Those who *support* a shift in paradigms are, like Randi Altschul, outsiders. They are individuals who have "operational naiveté," lack investment in the old paradigm and are tinkerers. Paradigm shifters are often called radical, out-of-touch, impractical or eccentric.

An example of this type of thinking is the story of Charles Kettering, a 20th century engineering industrialist. Kettering's labs were in Detroit, but his home was in Dayton, Ohio. This was also true for some of Kettering's colleagues, and on the weekends, they would often drive to their homes in Dayton. To get from Detroit to Dayton, they would take Route 25.

One day, a colleague said to Kettering, "I understand that you drive from here to Dayton in four and one-half hours. I'm a much better driver than you are, and I can't do it." Ever interested in offering scientific proof, Kettering offered the fellow a ride to Dayton that weekend. Sure enough, the trip took about four and a half hours. As they arrived, his passenger said, "Hell, no wonder you can do it. You didn't stay on Route 25!"[3]

Typically, the most well-known authorities in a field are the most outspoken practitioners of the old paradigm, the ones who dutifully drive Route 25. The least well-known are more likely to be promoters of a new paradigm, a new route, mainly because they have less invested in and less to gain from the old. Often, the fringe of a field provides fertile ground for innovations and manifestations of the "impossible."

It was Thomas Hobbes who said, "Had I read as much as others, I might have been as ignorant." James Watson, co-discoverer of DNA, said, "Well, you see, I was doing something my peers thought unwise; if they had thought it wise, they would have done it." In *The Prince*, Machiavelli writes,

> "There is nothing more difficult to carry out, nor more doubtful of success, nor more dangerous to handle, than to initiate a new order of things. For the reformer has enemies in all who profit by the old order, and only lukewarm defenders in all those who would profit by the new order."[4]

My goal for *Saving Black America* is a paradigm shift in civil rights, not notoriety. Besides, the civil rights movement, like most movements, inches forward based on the words and deeds of courageous spokespeople and, perhaps more importantly, on the actions of millions of lesser known activists. There is no dishonor in being counted among the latter group. So, I make no apologies for my relative anonymity. One of Dr. King's favorite poems, "Be the Best of Whatever You Are," includes the following lines:

> We can't all be captains, we've got to be crew,
> There's something for all of us here,
> There's big work to do, and there's lesser to do,
> And the task you must do is the near.[5]

Now, please note: *Saving Black America* is not about economics *per se*, it is not about "silver rights" as my friend Elder Eugene Johnson puts it. Propelling more Black Americans into the ranks of the middle class or the wealthy merely for the sake of doing so is not my motivation. More rich Black folk who have no empathy for their struggling brothers or sisters have no place on my list of priorities. There are legendary stories of wealthy and well-known Black people who have been treated like runaway slaves, and others who, if given the choice, would prefer to be White. No, the primary value of significantly increasing the accumulation of assets is to leverage them for the greater good of those most in need.

The subtitle of *Saving Black America* is "An Economic Plan for Civil Rights." Is it *not*, however, "A Plan for Economic Civil Rights." Key to the readers is the subtle difference to which noun the adjective "economic" modifies. It modifies "plan", not "civil rights."

Abraham Lincoln once said that if he could save the union without freeing the slaves, he would do so. I say that if I could discuss the next level of civil rights without mentioning economic development, I would do so. But just as emancipation was required to reach the goal of saving the union, so is economic development the *sine qua non* of civil rights in the 21st century. For me, economic development is not an end. It is a means to civil rights.

Saving Black America represents a paradigm shift that pleads with Black America to do the following:

(1) think deeply about the comparative status and conditions of our lives, especially about the lives of the least well-off among us,

(2) consider the structures — the internal and unstated rules which we observe — that guarantee continuation of overwhelmingly negative trends for our group,

(3) imagine a new set of rules, a new set of requirements necessary to reverse negative trends,

(4) develop a new plan, a new paradigm, for Black civil rights; and

(5) apply the paradigm to current problems.

You will note that the presentation of a proposed plan is listed fourth out of the above five steps above. You will also note from the Contents that my plan is presented in the 13th of 31 chapters. I believe that the reader's consideration of how we came to be where we are is as important as "Odom's plan." As viable as I believe my plan to be, what matters most is thinking deeply about how we came to this point in our history.

This introduction began with me recalling my beloved and belated father. I hasten to add that my belated mother, Rosa Grant Odom, is equally beloved.

Many years after having conceived the idea for this book and after having written an earlier version, I decided to retype the thousand or so of my father's sermons, which my mother sent to me after Reverend's passing in 1979. Deep in the box was one of his longest sermons: "Go, Buy for Yourselves."[6] This sermon is one of a very few in which its year of creation can be fixed. In the sermon, Reverend said "With the Supreme Court decision of May 17th last, why bother?" This reference meant that the sermon was given just after the landmark 1954 U. S. Supreme Court Brown v Topeka Board of Education decision. I have included "Go, Buy for Yourselves" as the 30th chapter of this book. While Reverend's sermon was not written for publication, nearly half a century later, I found it compelling and hope that you will also.

How

> "I will stand upon my watch, and set me upon the tower, and will watch to see what he will say unto me, and what I will answer when I am reproved. For the vision is yet for an appointed time, but at the end it shall speak and not lie: though it tarry, wait for it: for it will surely come, it will not tarry. And the Lord answered me and said, write the vision, and make it plain upon tablets, that he may run that readeth it."
>
> —Habakkuk 2:1–3

While considering why we need a dramatic shift in the civil rights movement, we also need to consider how to accomplish this. The most fundamental "how," contemplation, is known but is seldom practiced within the existing paradigm.

Contemplation through silence is greatly valued, especially the silence that represents a break in the action, that represents opportunities to reflect, regroup, restage, and restart. Most religions acknowledge silence or "meditation" as critical to spirituality. It is the time when one is most likely to hear from and feel the presence of God. Biblical examples of such times include prayer, fasting, travels, wilderness experiences, and retreats (to ships, temples, an upper room) for study, planning, and reflection. Through these breaks in daily activities, individuals, and groups gain direction, perspective, and wisdom.

In a wonderful little book, *Zen in the Martial Arts*,[7] author Joe Hyams tells the story of his audition to study under the great Bruce Lee. After Lee demonstrated his skills, he asked Hyams, "Do you realize you will have to unlearn all you have learned and start over again?" This question represents more than shallow rhetoric.

Lee then tells a story about a university professor who visited a Japanese master to inquire about Zen. It became clear to the master that the professor was much more interested in impressing him than he was in learning anything new. After listening patiently, the master offered tea to the professor. The master poured the tea, and when the professor's teacup was full, he continued to pour. As the tea overflowed the cup, the professor alerted the master to the mess he was making. The master said, "Like this cup, you are full of your own opinions and speculations. How can I show you Zen unless you first empty your cup?"

Cultured southerners have many sayings that help people learn appropriate behavior, including the importance and power of abstemiousness. One that comes to mind is this: "When one does not know what to say, know what to do!" Street folk have their own version, too: "You needs to go sit down somewhere!" Both sayings are calls for silence, for a break in the action.

Specifically, we need breaks from mindless protests, endless cycles of perceived victimization, tired sermons, old mental tapes (saying the same old lines we're supposed to say), and incoherent and self-deprecating rap music. We need breaks from Black-on-Black crime and embarrassing appearances on *Jerry Springer* and every court show on television in which we argue with everyone about everything. We need a break from selling out, from marching, picketing and sitting in, from grim-faced press conferences, from hopelessness, *from obsolete strategies* — just for a while so we can think, renew, regenerate and regain composure.

Silence in itself is not necessarily a positive. Some negatives that can come from silence include: indifference, laziness, lethargy, depression, confusion, scheming and fear. But there is a better silence.

This silence waits with anticipation and expectation. Dr. Robert Schuller says that when in the eye of the storm, do nothing, trust and wait.

Reverend once preached a sermon entitled, "A Long Patience[8]," based on II Samuel 18:22 "And David sat between the two gates..." The following are highlights of that wonderfully wise sermon.

> "If you have not acquired the art of patient wait-ing, you had better learn it at once, for you will have to spend much of your lifetime sitting be-tween two gates— waiting while the forces you have set in motion slowly work out the inevitable results... Patience is not inaction, impassivity or indifference... Patience is an ingredient of cour-age, serenity, self-control, successful living and true happiness... We need to be patient with the world in which we live. Fair weather today, and yet, at some hour, patience will be the virtue we shall need to exercise. Foul weather — patience will carry us through to an eventide of peace..."
> "Stormy days are ahead. Dark clouds threaten a deluge... Be not impassive, inactive or indiffer-ent. These times demand courage, steadfastness. This is a demand for patience."

> "We need to be patient with ourselves... Having done all, wait...the secret of attainment lies in patient striving and patient waiting... We need to be patient with others... We need to be patient with God. God took the long view... taking the long view will help us."

This book is the result of the long view — spanning 20 years. The book's seed was planted during an interaction in 1980 with a promi-nent civil rights leader. After his rousing speech, I asked about his next gig. He told me that he was joining Jesse Jackson for the 1980 March on Washington. *The 1980 March on Washington*! I naively asked "Why? What good will another March on Washington do?" Incensed, the other fellow launched into a tirade, which included a challenge to my Black-ness. Shocked at his personal attack, I strongly defended my Blackness, but offered only a weak defense of my question, primarily because I hadn't thought it through.

I sang in the concert choir while working on my undergraduate degree. I was both intrigued and challenged by the range of music — from sacred selections in Latin to spirituals. Although it has been more than 30 years since I graduated, a few songs still resonate. One of them was the soft and beautiful "Hush, No More." While I cannot recall all of lyrics, it began like this: "Hush, no more. Hush, no more, be silent. Be silent all."

After many hours of thought, several rewrites, dozens of conversations, and a few speeches, I have thought it through and now I offer this treatise. To get here, I had to hush. I emptied my cup several times, and I continue to do so.

I believe that my thoughts represent a unique perspective, and I trust that, in some way, it makes a contribution to the betterment of a wonderful people. This book is a study in patient striving and patient waiting — with anticipation. My goal is simple: to make a difference for Black people — whom I love. It is in that spirit that I entrust this work to you.

Division I
WHERE ARE WE?

CHAPTER 1

Dionte

Dionte Wilkins is six years old and Black *(yes, I said "Black" — see Appendix A)*. His mother registered him in first grade at Washington Elementary School today. Sound normal? Far from it. The date is November 17, and neither Dionte nor his siblings have ever attended school.

Dionte's mother, Shantel Collins, just arrived in Madison, Wisconsin from the Robert Taylor Homes of Chicago. She and her children are living temporarily with her aunt who preceded her to Madison by seven months. They and other relatives moved, they say, for a better, safer environment for their kids and better job opportunities.

Ms. Collins is an unemployed high school dropout. She is 22 years old and pregnant with her second child by a man who is not the father of Dionte. She has never married.

It is cold in Wisconsin and Dionte has no winter coat; but that is only one of his problems. Dionte Wilkins begins his public school experience years behind his peer group — many of whom have been reading for more than two years and have logged hundreds of computer hours. Not only has he never touched a computer, Dionte knows no alphabets or numbers. He cannot recognize the names of colors or shapes. He cannot hold a pencil properly, nor does he recognize his own name when it is written. It is as if a recently liberated slave child of 1865 had been beamed across time.

1

Dionte knows nothing of working cooperatively in groups, lining up, sitting still for an extended period of time, delaying gratification or waiting his turn. Dionte has had little "home training" and he is angry. He has a right to be.

Dionte has witnessed events that most adults will never see in their lives — a drive-by shooting, beatings, robberies, drug sales, and prostitution. He has learned from the adults around him to curse like a mule-skinner and to hit children.

Dionte has health problems. His mother received no pre-natal care and he was a low-birth weight infant. His mother also drank and smoked crack cocaine before she knew she was pregnant. She stopped using alcohol and drugs when she discovered she was pregnant, but she didn't stop smoking cigarettes. Dionte has an ear infection and five cavities. He has received some of his childhood inoculations, but not all of them.

It is the week before Thanksgiving and Dionte's family has no permanent place to live. On Thanksgiving Day, his family will rely on a shelter for dinner.

Dionte is no dummy. He can recite all the words to several "gangsta" rap cd's. And he's proud. He'll fight anybody who messes with him or looks at him funny.

Dionte will lag behind in school and "Trouble" will become his middle name — at school and in the community. His only sense of belonging will be found in a gang. His income will come from the sale of crack and robberies. His self-esteem will rise or fall on his physical prowess and his ruthlessness with guns, the number of babies he can sire by the number of women and girls, the length of his rap sheet and especially the number and the length of his prison stays.

On good days, Dionte dreams of living "large" as either a basketball player or rapper. On most days, he has no dreams at all.

Dionte will probably die early from one of any number of causes — a drug overdose, AIDS, heart disease, sclerosis of the liver, but most likely from a bullet wound. He will resent his life, hate people with money and feel affection for only the bloods of his gang.

Dionte is a composite representing millions of poor Black kids who are headed for unimaginable trouble because there is no bridge from where they are to where they must be to succeed.

Contemporary life for Black Americans has become a caricature of life for White Americans in which some demographics are similar, while Black negatives are vastly exaggerated — especially by the media Without a doubt, there are more rich and middle-class Black Americans than ever before. Virtually every industry has well-placed Black professionals who earn very respectable salaries. And in this era,

2

we are privileged to know of a handful of Black entrepreneurs who have broken through the concrete ceiling to become billionaires.

Despite this progress, life for poor Black Americans leaves much to be desired. Overall trends for Black vs. White Americans demonstrate significant negative difference for us. If one were to name a negative demographic in America, chances are, Black people lead.

Some Black trend trackers paint rosy pictures of Black America's future. They speak of the potential for business development, increasing numbers of Black professionals in key areas, and the continuous growth of annual Black gross national product. *Black Enterprise* and *Ebony* magazines do a superb job of providing hope and role models for Black Americans in search of examples, guidance, inspiration, and information. I too am buoyed by such information.

Focusing on Black successes is only half of the equation for improving overall life conditions for the majority of Black Americans. The other half requires squarely facing our negatives, just as effective medical treatment depends on an accurate diagnosis of a person's illnesses and prognoses based on life style. The following data, gathered from a variety of sources, provide such a diagnosis.

FAMILIES & DEMOGRAPHICS

1. In 1950, 78% of all Black families were headed by married couples. By 1996, only 34% of Black families were headed by married couples.[1]

2. The rate of low birth rate babies was the highest for any ethnic group and was twice the rate for White women.[2]

3. In 1995, the life expectancy of a White female was almost 80 years on average. For a White male, life expectancy was 73 years. For a Black female, it is about six years less, or 74, but Black males did not live to the typical retirement age of 66 — dying, on average, at age 64.7.[3]

4. The percent of White children who live with their grandparents is 4%, while 14% of Black children live with grandparents.[4]

5. Although Black teen birth rates have declined significantly since 1970, they remain twice the rate of White teens.[5]

6. In 1993, for the 15–24 year old group, there were 89 deaths per hundred thousand for White youths, but 162 deaths per hundred thousand for Black youths.[6]

7. In 1970, Blacks accounted for nearly 90% of all minorities in the U.S. By 1994, we were less than 50% of all minorities.[7]

8. Blacks are on the verge of becoming the second largest ethnic minority group.[8]

9. 40% of Black children live in poverty, and comprise more than 50% of the foster care system.[9]

10. Black children were more likely to live with two parents during slavery than they are today.[10]

HEALTH

11. Black women bear the largest breast cancer mortality burden in the nation[11].

12. Black men are more likely to die of heart disease than American Indian, Asian, Hispanic or White men.[12]

13. Black men are twice as likely as White men to die from prostate cancer.[13]

14. Blacks have the highest U.S. cancer rates.[14]

15. As compared to Whites, Black Americans are not receiving optimal asthma treatment.[15]

16. Elderly Blacks are far less likely than elderly Whites to get flu shots.[16]

17. By 1995, Black Americans had, by far, the highest percentage of AIDS cases — 92.6 per 100,000. The rate per 100,000 for Whites was 15.4; for Hispanics, it was 46.2; for American Indians, it was 12.3; and for Asians, it was 6.2.[17]

18. In 1994, 1 of every 3 deaths among young Black men between the ages of 25-44 was due to HIV related illnesses.[18]

19. In 1996, 11.5% of non-Hispanic White Americans were not covered by any form of health insurance, but for Black Americans it was 21.7%.[19]

20. The suicide rate among Black males more than doubled from 1980 to 1995.[20]

21. In 1995, the infant mortality rate for Black children was more than twice that of Whites.[21]

22. We represent more than 57% of new AIDS cases.[22]

23. Black men die at a 97% higher rate of stroke than do White men, and Black women die at a 71% higher rate than do White women.[23]

24. AIDS has become the leading killer of Black Americans between the ages of 25 and 44.[24]

25. 17.6% of White and 45.9 % of Black Americans have herpes.[25]

26. High blood pressure in Blacks is linked to perceiving racism and doing nothing to combat it.[26]

INCARCERATION

27. Between 1985 and 1995, the number of Black male prisoners with sentences of more than 1 year increased by 143% and the number of Black female prisoners rose by 204%. At the end of 1995, there were more Black males in state or federal prisons (510,900) than White males (493,700).[27]

28. At the end of 2000, approximately one-third of all Black males were involved with the penal institution.[28]

29. In 1995, the number of Black men enrolled in higher education was 556,000, but the number of Black men incarcerated in federal and state prisons and local jails was 711,600.[29]

30. The chance that a White man in the U.S. will spend some time in a state or federal prison during his lifetime is 2.5%, while the chance

that a Black man will spend similar time is 28.5%. The chance that a White woman in the U.S. will spend similar time is 0.5%, but for a Black woman, it is 3.6%.[30]

31. 51% of Black males can expect to be arrested for a felony sometime in their lives.[31]

32. In 1990, on an average day in America, 25% of all Black men between the ages of 20 and 29 were either in prison, jail, or on probation or parole.[32]

33. In 1991, the national incarceration rate in state and federal prisons for White males was 352 per 100,000; for Black males between the ages of 25 and 29, the rate was 6,301 per 100,000.[33]

34. In 1992, there were 14,000,000 arrests in America; 5,000,000 of them were Black males. At the time, there were only 5,500,000 Black males between the ages of 18 and 40.[34]

ECONOMICS

35. 98% of Black money is spent outside the Black community.[35]

36. Black net worth at the end of slavery in the 1860s was approximately 1.2% of the total. In 1998, it was approximately 1%.[36]

37. A dollar circulates in the American Asian community for up to 28 days before it is spent with outsiders. In the Jewish community, the circulation period is 19 days. In the WASP community it is 17 days. In the Black community, it is 6 hours.[37]

38. Under Pres. Clinton in 1999, poverty in the U.S. fell to its lowest level in two decades due to increases in the Hispanics and Whites populations. Nonetheless, the number of poor Blacks remained unchanged at 9.1 million.[38]

39. The income gap between Whites and Blacks increased in 1998.[39]

40. Black people own only 3% of the nation's businesses, while White men own 64%.[40]

EDUCATION

41. Although only 17% of the public school population, Black students constitute 37% of "at risk" students.[41]

42. The average number of hours of television watchers per week in White households is 49.8. In Black households, it is 73.1.[42]

43. The total number of doctorates awarded in 1996 in the fields of geometry, logic, number theory, astronomy, astrophysics, acoustics, nuclear chemistry, meteorology, geology, geochemistry, paleontology, mineralogy, geomorphology, hydrology, oceanography, marine science, engineering physics, engineering science, nuclear engineering, ocean engineering, petroleum engineering, systems engineering, biophysics, plant genetics, endocrinology and zoology was 1,605. Of this number, 0 were awarded to Black Americans.[43]

44. In math achievement, although they share the same schools, Asian American students are the best in the world, while Black American students are the worst in the world![44]

The legacy of poverty, racism, and discrimination has been inherited by the Diontes of the world. These children are often the victims of malnourishment, mental, physical and sexual abuse, poor parenting, abandonment, miseducation, murder, *in utero* drug addiction, and sexually transmitted diseases, including HIV. If emergency interventions do not occur, these young victims are likely to bequeath the same problems to their own children, thereby perpetuating the worst social trends. As stated earlier, the news is not all bad. As examples, high school graduation rates are up, crime and unwed pregnancy rates are down. Yet, small steps forward when catching up requires great leaps translates into "too little, too late."

Futurists and economists analyze raw data, and then project emerging trends. A prime example is Jeremy Rifkin's *The End of Work.*[45] Rifkin is the President of the Foundation on Economic Trends. The central theme of his book is that computerization is advancing so rapidly that the role of work in our lives will soon be transformed. Although most of our lives center around work, we will not be prepared for the shocking transformation. Young people are prepared from an early age to work. As adults, we work to earn and accumulate money. In our retirement, we live on the assets accumulated during our working years. Therefore, work is the central focus of our lives. Rifkin posits that automation is rapidly and surreptitiously replacing so many workers that billions of people world-wide will be able to add little value to the work that computerized machines can do cheaper and better. Consequently, machines will replace them.

In *The End of Work* is a chapter entitled "Technology and the African-American Experience."[46] The chapter chronicles the roles Black workers have played in the American enterprise, and how irrelevant Black labor, thereby, Black people have allegedly become. As slaves, share-croppers, and unskilled factory laborers, according to Rifkin, the large niches filled by Black workers have been eliminated by automation every time, by the automatic cotton picker or assembly line robotics. By 1970, the government employed 57% of all Black male college grads and 72% of all Black female grads. Furthermore, a high percentage of Black public sector jobs are dedicated to overseeing government programs for other Black people.

Rifkin cites Sidney Willhelm's 1970 book *Who Needs the Negro?*[47] to underline the trend of Black Americans' liberation from "[our] historical state of oppression into one of uselessness." Willhelm states,

> "An underestimation of the technological revolution can only lead to an underestimation of the concomitant racial revolution from exploitation to uselessness; to misjudge the present as but a continuation of industrialization rather than the dawn of a new technological era, assures an inability to anticipate the vastly different system of race relations awaiting the displaced Negro."[49]

Rifkin concludes that while a minority of Black leaders understand the pre-eminence of economics as the central cause of Black woes, most Black civil rights leaders are misdiagnosing of our problems. Traditional leaders in mainstream Black organizations continue to perceive the Black plight in strictly political terms, arguing that social discrimination is at the root of the crisis and that anti-discrimination laws were the appropriate cure.

> "Increasingly, he [the Negro] is not so much economically exploited as he is irrelevant... The dominant whites no longer need to exploit the black minority: as automation proceeds, it will be easier for the former to disregard the latter. In short, White America, by a more perfect application of mechanization and a vigorous reliance upon automation, disposes of the Negro; consequently, the Negro transforms from an exploited labor force into an outcast."[48]

8

Futurists are not astrologers. They track data trends to predict likely realities. The trends they project are based on the assumption that behavior patterns will go unchanged. Consequently, the predictions of Rifkin, Willhelm, and others are not God's will. The futures they describe for us are predictable only if we remain true to our current paradigm, our current pattern of doing things. And Rifkin's work in particular has drawn criticism for its draconian conclusions.

The work of futurists is more akin to Ebenezer Scrooge's graveside vision of the future. Given the life Scrooge led, the vision of a cold, lonely death seemed inevitable. The question that inspired Scrooge's awakening was, "Are these shadows of the things that *will be* or are they shadows of the things that *may be only*?"

Futurists are tracking shadows of the things that *may be* only, for they are incapable of determining what will be. Black Americans have proven that we are capable of profound group-wide normative change. We can produce more positive data to track and a more positive future to project. With the help of God, we can determine what will be.

There are two prevailing theories that attempt to explain our troubles. The first is that we are the perpetual victims of insidious, virulent and institutionalized racism. The adherents of this theory believe that we will always have to fight against racism, to remain angry, to seek protected class status and to obtain reparations. They do not want to acknowledge progress in the civil rights arena; they fear that White Americans might assume that their work in the area is done and shift priorities.

The other theory is that Black people are genetically inferior and simply cannot do better. Learned and lettered racists (to say nothing of the unlearned and unlettered ones who comprise their majority) have theorized that there are genetic limitations on how much Black Americans can learn. They believe that allocating resources specifically for our civil rights needs is a waste. They hold that violence, drug abuse and child abuse are endemic to the sub-species they believe us to be, and that educational failure, unemployment, incarceration, and ignorance are the products of congenital stupidity and laziness.

The racism theory is true, but since the signing of the 1964 Civil Rights Act, it's becoming increasingly false. Regarding the second theory, scholars have sufficiently debunked the flawed data and frankensteinian constructs pieced together to attempt to prove theories of racial inferiority/superiority. Intellectual racists cannot sufficiently isolate one racial group from another. Suffice it to say that rational Americans utterly reject those theories.

But there is a third theory. It is that our problems stem from our blind devotion to an aging and increasingly limited civil rights strategy.

This strategy has created a collective mindset in which we see ourselves as the world's permanently aggrieved darker member, compelled to protest for the rest of our days. Like Sisyphus, we are endlessly pushing the boulder of racial equity uphill. As a result, we are tired of pushing and our supporters are suffering from "empathy fatigue."

Our accomplishments in the 1960s were due less to our grassroots struggles and more to the success of an overarching model for change. It is critical that we understand:

1. The power of the model we created, which I name "the legislative-protest" model for civil rights;
2. The model's universal development over the past 20 years;
3. The model's dilution and demise;
4. How civil rights opponents have strategized against the model;
5. How it eventually has been rendered virtually useless.

Theories aside, truth is, no one knows what to do with Dionte — not his mother, his teacher, the school, the city, the state, the nation nor the civil rights movement. No societal sector is prepared to reverse what Lisbeth Schorr[50] calls the "rotten outcomes" that characterize Dionte's life. Our society is especially ill prepared to meet the needs of the millions of Black youth whom Dionte represents.

Saving Black America has an answer for Dionte and for his mother, Shantel. This book proposes a new model for Black civil rights. It offers rationales for changing from our legislative-protest model to an economically-based model, one that promotes self-reliance with "malice towards none." *Saving Black America* will support the belief that overcoming (as in "We shall...") is never a *fait accompli*, but a series of victorious battles in an ongoing war.

Saving Black America was written to make a difference for Dionte by urging the adoption and implementation of a new model for civil rights with *all deliberate speed* to assure the survival, safety and happiness of our entire group and, eventually, for the survival of the United States.

CHAPTER 2

Are Black Americans A Group?

A pre-requisite to developing a new model for Black civil rights is determining whether or not Black Americans constitute a group. As elementary as this may seem, our identity as a cultural, ethnic or racial group is increasingly being called into question, not only by White and Hispanic Americans, but also by many Black Americans.

From our brutal kidnapping to these shores until very recently, it was clear that we were a group, like it or not. The first American melting pot was the vile and violent pureeing of representatives of various African cultures and their tribes, languages and dialects, religions, customs, social structures, foods, attire, and norms. That a previously oppressed people — Americans — could conceive and perpetrate for centuries the cruelest form of slavery is beyond understanding. President and slave owner Thomas Jefferson even said that one hour of American Black slavery was worse than ages of the oppression against which White Americans rose in rebellion to oppose.

Black American slaves could never work themselves out of slavery. Laws that forbade teaching basic literacy to Black slaves ensured the systematic and permanent ignorance of their homeland, language, religion, culture, region, and family name. The system was so pervasive and devastating that it is virtually impossible for Black Americans to discover homeland regions of origin, family histories or even names. This is unique to Black Americans due to the pervasiveness and perniciousness of American slavery.

13

Some may be thinking, "Oh Lord, another Black man whining about the effects of slavery!" I will not argue against such a conclusion. I am whining about the effects of slavery, but not for predictable reasons.

It takes neither courage nor insight to declare that slavery should never have occurred in America. Even so, had the progenitors and guardians of the institution of American slavery observed any of the time-honored conventions of traditional slavery, including the ability to work one's way out, slavery would not have the lasting devastating effects that it does. Black slaves would have been permitted to know their roots. Armed with the heritage of our names, regions, cultures, languages, religions, customs, and scholarship our presence on these shores would not have resulted in a 400 year search for justice, identity and belonging. Such knowledge would have been a significant threat to the institution of slavery, but all of America would have been even more enriched by the contributions of Black Americans and by better understanding of the differences between African cultures that influence differences among Blacks.

Original cultural and tribal differences may account for many of the behaviors demonstrated by some Black Americans today. Many are unaware of the origins of those influences. Ancient tribal differences may explain modern differences in religious practices, family structures, traditions, gifts, and disease susceptibility. Then again, maybe not.

Whether because of necessity or the success of the slavery-imposed melting pot, Black Americans have, at times, worked cooperatively to achieve breakthroughs. Some of these historical events were slavery, the Civil War, Reconstruction, and the Jim Crow era.

However, the success of the civil rights movement gives us pause. In many ways, Black Americans were prepared to struggle but were unprepared to win. We won when laws ensuring the first class status of all citizens were passed. Unfortunately, the assassination of Dr. Martin Luther King, Jr. dissolved whatever unity we once enjoyed. Since then the African Diaspora has been divided.

A popular quote during Black History Month is "We are the descendants of kings and queens." And that is true for a few. Most of us are more likely descended from average folks. America's founding fathers are responsible for our enslavement, the perpetuation of racism and for our ignorance about our roots.

We must explore internecine differences because when we speak of Black Americans we are referring to the least and the great, from Maya Angelou to Marcus Wayne Chenault (the murderer of Mrs. Alberta King, Dr. King's mother), from Secretary of State Colin Powell to Colin Ferguson (the subway mass murderer).

"Are we or are we not a group?" is a fundamental question worthy of our attention. The easy answer is, "In spite of our differences, of course we are!" The more I read, listen and observe, however, the more I am convinced that we must talk among ourselves long and hard before taking another step. We are a group divided, and there are four forces, which work against group cohesion and action.

Black ultra-conservatives speak of impoverished, troubled Black people like Southern Whites speak of po' white trash. The notion seems to be, "We pulled ourselves up by our own boot straps, and they should too. And if *they* don't, it's their own fault and *they* deserve what *they* get!" From their perspective, this attitude is not "cold-hearted," it's the American way. It's what Dr. King meant by judging others "not by the color of their skin, but by the content of their character."

I could retire if I had $100 for every time I've heard some White person say, "I don't see differences. Everyone looks the same to me!" Aside from the idiocy of that statement, a growing number of African Americans are saying the same thing. Chief among them is Ward Connerly, the conservative California realtor and university regent who spearheaded the passage of California's Proposition 209, which ended Affirmative Action in the state. I have watched Connerly on CNN, C-Span and *60 Minutes,* and have come to the conclusion that he fancies himself a thick-lipped White man. Connerly does not believe that African Americans represent a group. We are just individuals who must swim or sink on individual merit.

In the old days, we had names for the likes of Connerly — e.g. sell out, handkerchief head, Uncle Tom, house nigger, WHM (White Man's Nigger). Today, his admirers (which include many Black Americans) call him refreshing, cutting edge, leader, even civil rights advocate and heir to Dr. King.

Similar to ultra-conservatives are Black escapists who see Blackness as something to get away from. The goal is "up and out," usually through entertainment or sports. Escapists believe that if they can just make enough money, they can escape the stigma of being poor and Black. Escapist Blacks really don't like being Black, and they think that money will spare them the inconvenience. There are many examples of rich and middle-class Black people who prefer to be something other than Black as indicated by their life-styles, communities, associates, and club memberships. Denial for escapists is as much a result of what individuals don't do as much as it is a result of what they do. And primary among the things they don't do is to work to improve conditions and opportunities for other Black Americans.

The ultimate insult is inflicted by the escapist charitable giver. A wealthy Black American writes a fat check to a Black charity and assumes a "holier-than-thou" posture. Such Black people are operating as kind White people who help the down-trodden Negroes. Big checks are being written for reasons of politics, prestige, guilt, influence and hush money.

Liberal integrationists believe that the essence of the civil rights movement was to fully integrate into the White power and cultural structure to such a degree that one's best friends, professional colleagues, fellow parishioners, golfing buddies, and in-laws are, for the most part, White. To some, this might sound like selling out, but for liberal integrationists, it is the height of what Dr. King meant by judging others "not by the color of their skin, but by the content of their character." Liberal integrationists believe that government policies and programs are the mother's milk of social change and that White liberals often know more about what it truly means to be Black than do many Black people.

Black predators, including violent gang members, drug pushers, and pimps, hate Black people and being Black. Their hatred of Black people is borne of self-hatred. The masses of Black people are thought of as stupid, niggers, whores, and player haters. Since "those people" ain't nothing but low life, there's nothing wrong with selling them dope while pimping, intimidating, abusing, ignoring, and killing them. This has nothing to do with Dr. King. This is "Dog eat dog!" "Catch a sucker, bump his head!"

Less obvious predators include professionals who assume equal opportunity, Affirmative Action, and diversity positions only to undermine the programs they were charged to promote.

These groups notwithstanding, my experience is that most Black Americans still feel that we are a group. We feel connected. We are proud when group members do well, and we feel shame when group members break laws and verbs. *Saving Black America* will treat Black Americans as a group, with notable exceptions and wide variations acknowledged and accounted for.

CHAPTER 3

The "Where Do We Go From Here?" Question

"Out of the mouth of babes and sucklings hast thou ordained strength because of thine enemies, that thou mightest still the enemy and the avenger."

—Psalm 8:2

Several Black authors and leaders have admonished us to make money and to use it for the benefit of Black Americans as a whole. Earl Graves, in his indispensable magazine *Black Enterprise*, has, for many years, admonished Black Americans to develop our money making and money management skills. Other authors have added their voices to the cause: Dennis Kimbro's *Think and Grow Rich: A Black Choice*[1] (a Black version of Napoleon Hill's classic work), Brooke Stephens' *Talking Dollars and Making Sense*[2], George Fraser's *Race for Success*[3], Robert Weems' *Desegregating the Dollar*[4], and Robert Woodson's *On the Road to Economic Freedom*[5] have made valuable contributions.

But is the message being heard among Blacks, especially young people? The answer is "no."

Wealth gurus are virtually unanimous in the belief that wealth is a tangible manifestation of a spiritual or subconscious change. During the early 1900's, Napoleon Hill was hired by Henry Ford to interview the richest Americans of the day to determine their wealth-building secrets.

Despite the positive messages of Napoleon Hill, Ida B. Wells, Marcus Garvey, Charles Hamilton Houston, A. G. Gaston, Robert Woodson, and Earl Graves, negative attitudes persist among Black Americans about our collective ability to become financially secure.

The root of our defeatist attitudes are found in slavery. A 400-year history of enforced physical and psychological dependence persists. White Americans, through the government, undermined Black independence by reneging on commitments made during the Reconstruction era, through seventy years of *de facto* and *de jure* Jim Crow "separate but equal" discrimination laws, and through the addictive, albeit well-intentioned, social programs of the Great Society. In addition, *and more importantly*, Black American leaders have neither developed nor promulgated group-wide wealth building practices and norms alongside the well developed protest practices and norms.

Suze Orman in her bestseller *Nine Steps to Financial Freedom*[6] demonstrates that she shares the belief that the right attitude is prerequisite to financial success. For the 1998-99 season, Oprah Winfrey dedicated shows to sharing Orman's success formulas with Americans. In Oprah's January 18, 1999 show, Ms. Orman decided to teach her tough love, change-your-attitude money strategy to a culturally diverse group of teenagers. Oprah played videotaped excerpts of Orman's meeting with the teens. In the meeting, Orman pledged an amount to the teens on the provision that the allocation of the funds would be the result of a group decision. The teens could choose one of the following three options:

1. Orman would pay off one of the group member's debts.
2. They could give the money to one charity.
3. They could create a third option.

Orman gave two reasons when asked by Oprah why she would issue such a challenge. The first was that one motivated group member had said earlier, "If somebody gave me money, I wouldn't take it. I want to do it on my own." The second reason was that, in life, we must negotiate money priorities with a spouse and with business associates, so she believed that these kids needed to learn the lesson now.

Two hours of dialogue among the teens produced no decisions. Within the group a persuasive young Black teen pressed hard to be the recipient of the money. She said,

> "I don't think it's anything wrong with needing help and that's why we're here. And not so as I need anybody to pay my bills, but I need a loan or something.

18

> My child cannot even go to school because I am so
> far in debt. I owe $500, $600 in tuition. He can't go
> back to school and I can't work because he needs to
> be in school so I need help. I'm telling America,
> yes, I need help."[7]

This was profound. One of Orman's teachings was that giving money to a person who had not changed attitudes or habits would mean enabling bad habits and postponing the inevitable. Other group members stated that they did not want to give the money to this young woman primarily because they felt that she stubbornly refused to change her attitudes and behaviors.

But Orman's teachings and the disapproval of colleagues apparently meant little to this young woman. She persisted in her attitude of helplessness. Not only that, she took advantage of the moment to appeal directly to the nation for help.

Oprah added, "I would give you the money, but I know it won't do any good... it's about self-esteem... I've paid off people's bills: I've paid off friends' bills.... and they always end up back in debt."[7] Still undeterred, the young woman pressed on:

> "My thing is — I just need — like, I'm looking for
> a loan. I — I need help. I mean, I know people in
> this audience — I really, truly need help. My son
> can't — I mean, I need him to go to school so I can
> work."[8]

Orman retorted, "Yes. If you want people to help you, you have got to first help yourself."

Then, an interesting thing happened. The young woman's well-groomed and attractive mother was in the audience and she had comments:

> "... [my daughter] helps herself. I'm a living wit-
> ness. She does everything possible...She's been look-
> ing for jobs...I'm a single parent. [My daughter] is
> a single parent. So we have to have some kind of
> network in there to watch the children. I work af-
> ternoons. She has to work — she has a six year old
> brother also. So someone has to be at the home when
> we're not there... when she is working."[9]

This brief exchange on Oprah is important. The young woman felt such a lack of power that she felt a loan was the answer to her problems. This teen and her mother chose a $500.00 loan over direct financial advice from America's wealthiest Black citizen and a leading financial motivator.

This story is included not to ridicule this family. Their honesty and concern for their children are laudable. Rather, I include this story for what it represents — millions of Black people who feel as economically trapped as this mother and daughter, and as justified in their attitudes. It's as if we are saying, "Don't teach me to fish, GIVE ME A FISH!"

And poor Black people are not alone in feeling dependent on White people for financial support. Black multimillionaires can have the same feelings.

On April 14, 1998, ESPN televised "Sports and Race: Running In Place?"[11] The program was an outgrowth of President Clinton's Initiative on Race. Participants included President Clinton and an illustrious panel of individuals involved in sports, including former football superstar Jim Brown; John Thompson, then coach of the Georgetown University basketball team; Carmen Policy, owner of the San Francisco 49ers; Keyshawn Johnson, then stand-out receiver for the New York Jets; Jackie Joyner-Kersee, Olympic track gold medallist; Dennis Green, coach of the Minnesota Vikings football team; John Moores, owner of the San Diego Padres baseball team; Joe Morgan, baseball Hall of Famer and announcer; and Vince Dooley, Athletic Director of the University of Georgia.

During the give-and-take of the discussion, Keyshawn Johnson turned the tables by asking the following question of White panelists:

> "I want to ask a couple of powers that be — the athletic director, the owner of the Padres, and Mr. Policy — like, when I'm done playing professional sports I want to know when you guys are going to put something together to — not only do we put money in your pocket as players, but when it's all over and said and done, put us in a position to be the vice president of your team or in a power position to help other minorities out."[11]

It was clear that Keyshawn Johnson is an articulate Black professional athlete who is very dedicated to his people. Yet, if he remains healthy, his earnings will easily exceed $100 million to say nothing of his investments. In addition, he works with many other similarly situated Black men. Yet, his question of White panelists was, "Will you give us a job?"

A job?! What of ownership? What of creating jobs for others who follow behind? Jim Brown was the voice in the wilderness, having to argue with two outspoken Black panelists about Black independence through ownership. It was Brown who said,

> "It isn't a matter of a chance of acquiring a team.
> It's a matter of amassing the amount of dollars. And
> I'm sure that any African American group today that
> raised enough money could purchase a team... We
> talk about chance and opportunity and being allowed,
> yet our economic dollars are never pooled in a man-
> ner to give us that kind of power."[12]

I agree with Jim Brown, Oprah Winfrey, and Suze Orman. It is a pervasive sense of helplessness, not the lack of money that is the major part of the problem. There is also a collective confusion over strategy; in other words, how should we proceed? We must overcome helplessness and confusion.

There was much confusion at the 1998 National Bar Association Convention. On July 29, 1998, C-Span televised a controversial appearance by Supreme Court Justice Clarence Thomas before the annual convention of the National Bar Association in Memphis, Tennessee. The National Bar Association, comprised primarily of Black attorneys and judges, was founded years ago because of the American Bar Association's refusal to admit Black lawyers.

Later on July 29, the National Bar Association's agenda called for a reaction panel to the Thomas speech. I watched for an hour and 15 minutes as different lawyers spoke against Thomas' positions and decisions. The panel began with articulate, impassioned and learned opposition to Thomas from the late Judge Leon Higginbotham. Other panelists weighed in with their comments.

I was more than halfway into this program when I began to wonder why I had committed the time to watch it. The answer came at the very end (as the late Rev. James Cleveland sang "Lord, help me to hold out...").

Convention delegates were encouraged to ask questions of the panel. As you might expect of a group of lawyers, most questions were speeches that ended with some version of "What you think of what I just said?" Chairperson, Atty. Shelvin Louise Marie Hall was drawing the event to a close when she made a last minute acknowledgement of a young lawyer whom she referred to as Attorney Shabazz, who asked the following question:

> "I'm legal counsel and I represent the Million Youth
> March which will be taking place on Saturday, Sep-
> tember 5 (1998) in Harlem, New York City, and I
> travel all around the country organizing college stu-
> dents and young people in preparation for this event.
> And in general, what they have been expressing to
> me is that they are dissatisfied with the level of unity

of Black leadership. And as we approach this question, I'm trying to see is... how can the brilliance of the legal minds that we have, and the political figures that we have, the Black activists... it seems to be a lack of a coherent policy, a lack of unity that speaks to a lack of empowerment and leaves us continuously frustrated in our quest to solve the dilemmas that we face.

So that's my question today. What is the, what is your opinion on a comprehensive policy and strategy that can be engaged in by Black leadership to confront the problems we face?"[13]

Young Attorney Shabazz nailed it! *That is the question!* Many have considered it, but few have answered it. Where is the comprehensive strategy by Black leadership that we can implement to solve the problems we face?

The response to Attorney Shabazz reflects two devastating realities. The first is that panelists did not fall over each other to articulate their enthusiasm for their shared vision, mission, goals and strategies of the contemporary civil rights movement. The second is that intelligent, articulate, highly educated Black Americans *have no answer to the most important question of our time!* Panel moderator and Harvard Law Professor Charles Oglethorpe responded by discussing the founding of the National Bar Association, the National Civil Rights Museum, and the Million Youth March. As the din of weary applause died down, the program ended, the panelists and delegates dispersed, but Attorney Shabazz' unanswered question lingered like a spirit.

I greatly admire Professor Oglethorpe, but how much better it would have been if he had said the following:

"Great question! Unfortunately, I don't have an answer for you right now. We need a coherent strategy, but it is clear, that we don't have one. The differences today between Justice Thomas and his detractors are but one sign of our scattering in the wilderness. We have a similar lack of coherence in our approaches to practically everything, including education, criminal justice and incarceration, welfare, child-rearing, and economic development."

"One thing I know for sure, and that is that our old civil rights strategies are woefully insufficient to deal with the formidable challenges that face us. Although marching can serve as temporary fix, it is not a sufficient substitute for developing the plan to which you allude. Marching can't create money."

22

The "Where Do We Go From Here?" Question

"Let your Million Youth March be our last one. When you return from Harlem, let us sit down and think deeply about where we, as a people, need to be and plan how we will get there."

Since no one on the panel of learned lawyers said this to the Black youth of America, I say it to you.

CHAPTER 4

Leadership Responsibility

Millions of Black Americans know that, for decades, we have needed a new direction. Moreover, several thinking Black Americans have said so. Several books and articles have been written on the topic of where Black America should be headed and how to get there. I have learned much and have been personally motivated by my research.

Who is responsible for change? Depending on who you talk to, there are at least five answers. Change is the primary responsibility of:

individual Black Americans

groups of Black Americans

certain Black Americans

Black Americans as a whole

the government

Let us briefly explore each one of these categories.

Individual Black Americans. This philosophy holds that individuals are the masters of their own fate, that the time for excuses is over. Although we may not completely enjoy the benefits of social and economic equality, we can make dramatic improvements in our personal and family security, thereby improving our lives and our relationships with other ethnic groups. George C. Fraser is an excellent example of this philosophy of personal improvement. In *Race for Success* he urges individuals to "… listen, learn and join in"[1] the movement for Black economic independence. Fraser exhorts Black people to "pick what excites and moves you, search for and discover your purpose and passion in life, and then start down a new path."[2] In fairness, it must be said that although George Fraser endorses individual action, he has developed and maintains the largest Black international network to support positive individual activity. "There are a thousand helping hands waiting for you, but you must leap first, and the net with appear."[3]

Supporting individual changes, financial planner, investment advisor, and author Brooke Stephens minced no words in her book *Talking Dollars and Making Sense: A Wealth Building Guide for African Americans*[4] when she wrote,

> "The bottom line is that most black folks are scared of money. Scared to talk about it. Scared to admit that they don't understand it. Scared to take risks as entrepreneurs. Scared to let go of some of the old ideas that have kept us stuck in poverty. Scared to challenge outdated beliefs about prosperity and economic well-being. Scared to stop blaming racism for all the financial problems that exist in the black community."[5]

Brooke Stephens takes Black America to the financial wood-shed for our collective financial ignorance and inactivity. Ms. Stephens' observations and recommendations are well-founded.

Professor Shelby Steele in his much acclaimed *The Content of Our Character: A New Vision of Race in America*[6] also argues for individual responsibility for racial change, but Steele's goal appears to be that of cultural assimilation rather than overall improvement of the Black condition. Steele says,

> "Seeing for innocence pressures blacks to focus on racism and to neglect the individual initiative that would deliver them from poverty — the only thing that finally delivers anyone from poverty. With our eye on innocence we see racism everywhere and miss opportunity even as we stumble over it."[7]

Groups of Black Americans. This strategy draws its power from collective action, especially from "grass roots" organizations. These groups work to improve their organizations and communities. In *On the Road to Economic Freedom*[8], Robert L. Woodson strongly advocates a philosophy and strategy of small group actions for our own problems.

> "Blacks are at a turning point in history. The era of the great civil rights marches is over...Old strategies have run their course... It is time to approach the needs of the black underclass from a different perspective... [r]ather than accept solutions parachuted in by middle-class, professional service providers, black America must recognize and expand on indigenous, self-help neighborhood efforts."[9]

Certain Black Americans. Those "certain" Black Americans are usually Black leaders and intelligentsia. They are Dr. W. E. B. DuBois' "talented tenth." Those who are blessed with the gifts, skills, and opportunity to conceptualize a better world for Black Americans are compelled to do so, and to do so in ways that are practical.

Dr. DuBois says that "The Negro race, like all races, is going to be saved by its exceptional men. The problem of education... is the problem of developing the Best of this race that they may guide the mass away from the contamination and death of the Worst, in their own and other races."[10]

Andrew Young challenged an assembly of the National Association of Securities Professionals with these words, "You are [today's] Civil Rights Movement... Now we're trying to integrate the money. You're at the forefront of the movement for equality."[11]

Among those who hold that the responsibility for change rests on the shoulders of the talented ten percent is Marian Wright Edelman. She dropped the hydrogen bomb when she said, "All of our Mercedes Benzes and Halston frocks will not hide our essential failure as a generation of Black "haves" who did not protect the Black future during our watch."[12]

Black Americans as a whole. Virtually every banquet and conference speaker admonishes the masses. Rev. Jesse Jackson, Minister Louis Farrakhan, and other members of the clergy speak often and long about our collective plight and our shared responsibility for change. Now, the contents of each speech to Black Americans can vary greatly, but the common bond under this heading is that all Black Americans share (equal) responsibility for renorming the group.

Dr. Mary Frances Berry succinctly articulated the message this way:

> "We have hard realities to face within the Black community: finding ways to improve K-12 education,

to amass capital and increase entrepreneurship, to improve health care, which should include confronting the scourge of AIDS, and to step up efforts to provide opportunity generally for poor African-Americans."[13]

In his highly acclaimed book *Race Matters*[14], Professor Cornell West declares,

"What is to be done? How do we capture a new spirit and vision to meet the challenges of the post-industrial city, post-modern culture, and post-party politics?... the major challenge is to meet the need to generate new leadership. The paucity of courageous leaders... requires that we look beyond the same elites and voices that recycle the older frameworks."[14]

West goes on to add group nihilism — a sense pervasive sense of hopelessness and despair — that can only be controlled through conversion to a love ethic.

Professor Robert E. Weems, Jr., concludes his indispensable book *Desegregating the Dollar: African American Consumerism in the Twentieth Century*[15], with this statement:

"Black consumers, who now spend the vast majority of their money in shiny downtown and suburban shopping malls, enhance the economic bases of these outside areas to the detriment of their own enclaves... the future demands the development of strategies that will stimulate more constructive economic activity with the black community. A truly free people possess the power to produce, as well as to consume."[16]

The government. Voices that call for big government solutions to our problems are now few, weak, and hoarse. The advocates of Great Society-type programs have been on the offensive since the election of President Ronald Reagan in 1980. Nonetheless, it is widely held that laws and government policies continue to be the most powerful panaceas to past and present discriminatory practices.

While leading diversity education sessions, I explain the nature of institutional "isms" (racism, sexism, etc.) by posing rhetorical questions such as, "If you wanted to collect dust in your homes or dandelions in your yards, what should you do?" The obvious answer is "nothing." Dust particles and dandelion seeds are one with the environment. They are invisible and omnipresent, just as are ignorance, diseases, sin, and bigotry. These represent the natural state of things. Clean houses, green lawns, enlightenment, health, Godliness, and fairness are the results of intentional effort and hard work.

Units of government, be they national, state, county, or municipal are neither benign nor innocent in the matters of racial discrimination. In his profound and often frightening book *Search and Destroy: African-American Males in the Criminal Justice System*[17], Jerome G. Miller, says,

> "The national attempt to deal with a wide array of economic, social and personal problems through criminal justice processing has brought social disaster to our cities. If we are to make progress, we will need a new paradigm. It will be possible only when we begin handling most "criminalizable" incidents outside the criminal justice system altogether."[18]

My View

I agree with the spirit of most of the writers cited above. There are several points of attack in the war of "catch up" for Black Americans, and some points are more critical than others. My main concern is that not only is there no plan of attack, the most critical point of attack is not on the map.

Before proceeding to identify the critical missing category of thought, I hasten to say that I agree with Stephens, Fraser, Berry, DuBois, Edelman, and Miller. The onus falls on each Black American to get our financial act together, lead other Black Americans out of mendicancy, and pressure governmental agencies to rid themselves of racist practices and to treat Black Americans equitably. While the government should continue to combat racism in our society, government cannot develop the overall plan or lead in its implementation.

Fraser and Stephens write truth, and their strategy of financial planning, accounting, saving, and investing through delayed gratification is sober and right. When all is said and done, individual financial responsibility will set us free. Getting Black Americans to face this truth is the challenge. Although many of the financial barriers faced by Black Americans are perceived, they are firmly embedded in our minds. Convincing us differently is a gargantuan task.

As marketers and media moguls know well, perception equals reality. Until our perceptions of reality change, we will never get to the heart of creating wealth, individually and collectively. Helplessness, futility, and racism warp our perceptions; a strategic vision helps us to see our economic situation in a more empowering light.

While this concise observation is dead on, Dr. Berry's analysis demonstrates the confusion in the Black community regarding the remedy to our vexatious and pernicious problems. She says, "Our experiences of interactions between African-Americans and Whites are at the heart of our nation's racial woes."[19]

Black Americans do not come to the Race Negotiations Table as an equal. Rather, we choose to come as beggars or as pouting, demanding brats. Black America is not yet a skilled negotiator.

Superb plans are the products of superb planners. Cutting edge thinkers, civil rights leaders, Black business leaders, and academics must engage in a strategic planning process to develop our renaissance plan. This work must begin and be implemented soon.

> "Blow the trumpet in Zion, sanctify a fast, call a solemn assembly: Gather the people, sanctify the congregation, assemble the elders, gather the children... Spare thy people, O Lord, and give not thine heritage to reproach, that the heathen should rule over them..."
>
> —Joel 2:15–17

CHAPTER 5

A Letter to Black America

Black America must adopt new behaviors, a new civil rights strategy, to create Black wealth. That point was made by the following anonymous and apocryphal letter found on the Internet.

Dear Black Americans:

After all of these years and all we have been through together... it's appropriate for us to show our gratitude for all you have done for us.

We have chastised you, criticized you, punished you, and in some cases even apologized to you, but we have never formally nor publicly thanked you for your never-ending allegiance and support to our cause. This is our open letter of thanks.

We will always be in debt to you for your labor. You built this country and were responsible for the great wealth we still enjoy today. Upon your backs, laden with the stripes we sometimes had to apply for disciplinary reasons, you carried our nation.

We thank you for your diligence and tenacity. Even when we refused to allow you even to walk in our shadows, you followed close behind believing that someday we would come to accept you and treat you like men and women.

We publicly acknowledge Black people for raising our children, attending to our sick, and preparing our meals while we were occupied with the trappings of the good life.

Even during the times when we found pleasure in your women and enjoyment in seeing your men lynched, maimed and burned, some of you continued to watch over us and our belongings. We simply cannot thank you enough.

Your bravery on the battlefield, despite being classified as three-fifths of a man, was and still is outstanding. We often watch in awe as you went about your prescribed chores and assignments, sometimes laboring in the hot sun for 12 hours, to assist us in realizing our dreams of wealth and good fortunes.

Now that we control at least 90 percent of all of the resources and wealth of this nation, we have Black people to thank the most. We can only think of the sacrifices you and your families made to make all of this possible.

You were there when it all began, and you are still with us today, protecting us from those Black people who have the temerity to speak out against our past transgressions.

Thank you for continuing to bring 95% of what you earn to our businesses.

Thanks for buying our Hilfigers, Karans, Nikes, and all of the other brands you so adore.

Your super-rich athletes, entertainers, intellectuals, and business persons (both legal and illegal) exchange most of their money for our cars, jewelry, homes and clothing. What a windfall they have provided us!

The less fortunate among you spend all they have at our neighborhood stores, enabling us to open even more stores. Sure, they complain about us, but they never do anything to hurt us economically.

Allow us to thank you for not bogging yourselves down with doing business with your own people. We can take care of that for you.

You just keep doing business with us. It's safer that way. Beside, everything you need, we make anyway, even Kente cloth. You just continue to dance, sing, fight, get high, go to prison, backbite, envy and distrust and hate one another.

Have yourselves a good time, and this time we'll take care of you. It's the least we can do, considering all you've done for us. Heck, you deserve it, Black people.

For your labor, which created our wealth, for your resisting the messages of trouble-making Blacks like Washington, Delany, Garvey, Bethune, Tubman, and Truth, for fighting and dying on our battlefields, we thank you.

And we really thank you for not reading about the many Black warriors who participated in the development of our great country. We thank you for keeping it hidden from the younger generation. Thank you for not bringing such glorious deeds to our attention.

A Letter to Black America

For allowing us to move into your neighborhoods, we will forever be grateful to you. For your unceasing desire to be near us and for hardly ever following through on your threats due to our lack of reciprocity and equity — we thank you so much.

We also appreciate your acquiescence to our political agendas, for abdicating your own economic self-sufficiency, and for working so diligently for the economic well-being of our people. You are real troopers.

And, even though the 13th, 14th, and 15th Amendments were written for you and many of your relatives died for the rights described therein, you did not resist when we changed "Black rights" to "civil rights" and allowed virtually every other group to take advantage of them as well.

Black people, you are something else! Your dependence upon us to do the right thing is beyond our imagination, irrespective of what we do to you and the many promises we have made and broken. But, this time we will make it right, we promise. Trust us.

Tell you what, you don't need your own hotels. You can continue to stay in ours. You have no need for supermarkets when you can shop at ours 24 hours a day. Why should you even think about owning more banks? You have plenty now. And don't waste your energies trying to break into manufacturing. You've worked hard enough in our fields.

Relax. Have a party. We'll sell you everything you need. And when you die, we'll even bury you at a discount. How's that for gratitude?

Finally, the best part. You went beyond the pale and turned your children over to us for their education. With what we have taught them, it's likely they will continue in a mode similar to the one you have followed for the past 45 years (since school desegregation).

When Mr. Lynch walked the banks of the James River in 1712 and said he would make us a slave for 300 years, little did we realize the truth of his prediction. Just 13 more years and his promise will come to fruition. But with two generations of your children having gone through our education systems, we can look forward to at least another 50 years of prosperity. Things could not be better — and it's all because of you. For all you have done, we thank you from the bottom of our hearts. Black Americans, you're the best friends any group of people could ever have!

Sincerely,

All Other Americans

Although I am confident that this epistle was written by a very insightful Black American, its message requires only one additional comment — "Amen!"

CHAPTER 6

History of the Current Model: Charles Hamilton Houston

"When Brown against the Board of Education was being argued in the Supreme Court... [t]here were some two dozen lawyers on the side of the Negroes... [O]f those... lawyers... only two hadn't been touched by Charlie Houston... [T]hat man was the engineer of it all... if you do it legally, Charlie Houston made it possible..."[1]

- Thurgood Marshall

Ask the average American, "Who was the master mind behind the current civil rights movement?", the predictable response would be Dr. Martin Luther King, Jr. The truth is that while Dr. King was the drum major, Professor Charles Hamilton Houston founded the band. If Dr. King was Joshua, Charles Hamilton Houston was Moses.

Dr. Genna Rae McNeil's book, *Groundwork: Charles Hamilton Houston and the Struggle for Civil Rights*[2], provides excellent insight into the life of this obscure American hero. Houston, a Black man, son of a lawyer and a hairdresser, was born in 1895. He graduated Phi Beta Kappa in 1915 from Amherst University, became an instructor at Howard University at the age of 19, and served during World War I in a new Colored Army Officers Corp (instead of becoming a grunt in a Jim Crow unit).

After the war, Houston graduated in the top five percent of his class at Harvard Law School and was the first director of the NAACP

Legal Defense Fund (LDF), where he decided that education would be the LDF's primary focus. He then argued and won four carefully selected, precedent-setting civil rights cases before the U.S. Supreme Court (1938–1948).

Houston attempted to motivate the masses by informing them of his work. He laid the groundwork for victory in the 1954 Supreme Court case, *Brown v. Topeka Board of Education*, although he died of a heart attack four years earlier.

During the early years, Professor Houston had to answer the question, "How can Black people achieve equal rights nonviolently?" In the early 1930's, he realized that he had two options: legal protest or economic self-help. The choice he made altered the history of the United States dramatically and forever.

Houston focused his background, training, interests, and skills changing the racist laws of America. Legal redress was chosen with the full knowledge that the economic route was also a viable one, but before educational, employment, and wealth-building opportunities could be assured to Black Americans, the laws of the land had to reflect the first-class citizenship rights of all Americans and compensate for the centuries of disadvantage imposed on Black Americans. Professor Houston understood that Black Americans could not prosper economically while discrimination was legal.

Houston's strategies were developed, expanded, enhanced, and popularized by Dr. King and others to such a degree that a model of transformational change emerged in the 1960's and 1970's.

CHAPTER 7

The Current Model

I call the current civil rights model the "legislative-protest" model. A description of the model's 13 stages follows.

1. Some group members (typically activists and scholars) recognize an onerous state of affairs.

2. The founders of the movement work to achieve change through legal appeals designed to guarantee constitutional rights.

3. Founders of the movement extol the group's uniqueness through an increasing number of public statements.

4. Mass support surfaces for these statements and urges the movement founders forward.

5. Militant activities (including demonstrations, literature, proclamations, manifestos, demands, maybe violence) emerge.

6. The masses of the group become aware of the revolution and support it.

7. Some civil rights legislation is passed.

8. The body politic increasingly accepts the changes.

9. Group members assume token positions within the system.

10. The movement grows in number and influence in systems.

11. The movement's activities change, from working loudly from outside systems to working quietly within systems.

12. The movement experiences a period of quietude and confusion as it attempts to determine how onerous is the present state of affairs.

13. If necessary, repeat steps 1–12.[1]

This model is uniquely Black American. The model has been replicated worldwide, from Johannesburg to Tianamen Square, and, in my opinion, is a model second in importance only to the revolutionary model that caused the founding of the United States. Its crowning glory was the signing of the 1964 Civil Rights Act.

Not long after the signing of the 1964 Act, it became clear that civil rights had gained significant momentum. As a result, Black Americans received a small slice of the American pie in the form of entitlement programs and grants. This model was first explained by the Rev. Dr. Robert Terry, a White civil rights activist.[2]

Illustration 1

Other groups that had been relatively quiet began to implement our model for themselves. Other groups which had not previously seen themselves as minority groups saw benefits in becoming so. For example, Black, Jewish, Catholic and Indian groups were active during the civil rights movement, while Hispanic and Asian Americans were comparatively inactive — choosing instead to pursue an assimilationist strategy.

In addition, the women's movement became re-energized in the 1960's, and eventually feminists staged a linguistic takeover by phrasing protected classes as "women and minorities." Women demanded their slice of the American pie.

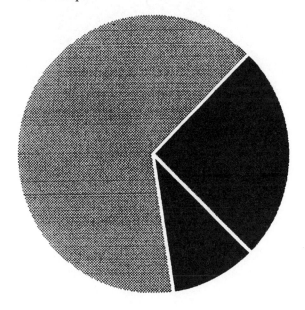

Illustration 2

In response to the demand, the powers-that-be quickly developed a counter strategy. The response was to appear to accede to demands, and then to proceed to slice the pie as follows.

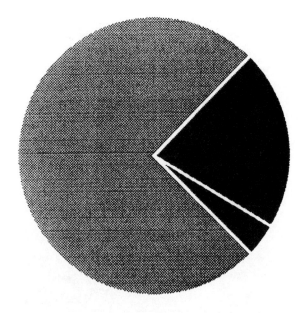

Illustration 3

The Current Model

Obviously, this division of the pie was disturbing to Black Americans and women.

Many different groups began using the model: ethnic groups (Hispanic Americans, Native Americans, and Asian Americans), older Americans (the Gray Panthers, predecessors of the powerful and respectable American Association of Retired Persons), and persons with disabilities. The last group successfully lobbied for and won the signing of the Americans with Disabilities Act of 1990. On the other hand, gays and lesbians have not been so successful, but continue to struggle to become acknowledged as a legitimate minority group.

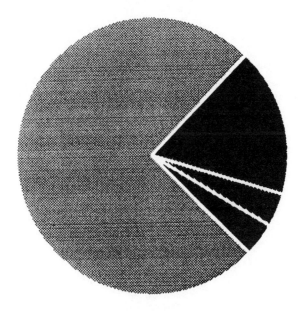

Illustration 4

The most fascinating and devastating use of the model was by the very group that had been the object of protest by all the other groups — White males. Eventually, a movement emerged to provide civil rights to White males. Groups were formed, including the National Association for the Advancement of White People and the chimerical "SPONGE" (Society for the Prevention of Negroes from Getting Everything). The progenitors of the movement created new terms like "White Power," "anti-reverse discrimination," and "anti-quota" clauses. White males had become a minority group, which begs the question, "If White males represent an aggrieved minority group, who controls the rest of the pie?"

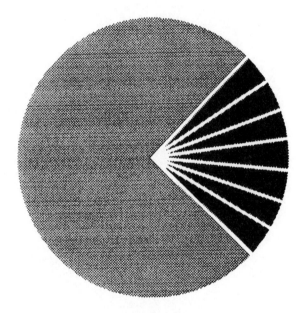

Illustration 5

The Current Model

A conspiracy theory about the death of the model posits that the enemies of civil rights purposefully overburdened the model with bogus minority groups to render it ineffective. More likely is the fact that people of all groups are in continual search of answers. Since few viable, cutting-edge models exist, we resort to whatever models have proven, over time, somewhat viable — which is why some depraved souls cannot allow Nazism or Soviet Communism to die.

The legislative-protest model is *not* dead, nor should it die, but it has been in irreversible decline for several years. As a result, the model should become a secondary strategy for Black people.

To relegate the contemporary model to a secondary position begs the critical question, "What will replace it?" Professor Houston and the NAACP knew the route to the new model in the 1930's — the route of economic development.

The notion that Black people must become oriented towards economic self-help is so commonly held that it is axiomatic. The central problems for contemporary Black America are two:

1. Economic development is seen primarily as something that only concerns business-oriented individuals.

2. Economic development is not seen as a civil rights strategy — the logical progression of the legislative-protest strategy of the civil rights movement.

In many ways, it appears as if Black Americans have an aversion to wealth accumulation. The time and energy that could be directed toward economic self-help is consumed by swings between anomie and protest. Strategically, Black America is like a person with two unmatched arms — one with magnificently developed biceps and triceps, the other withered from lack of use. We have honed protest to such a fine degree that public officials dare not offend us. Yet, our strategies for economic development are so infantile that a minority of us understand the need for an economically based structure, let alone having such a structure in place.

Our economic development arm is in dire need of therapy for it to have its size and strength match the legislative-protest arm. With two powerful arms, Black Americans can embrace our own problems and solve them. With two powerful arms, one can hold children, comfort the aged, free the imprisoned, and lift the bars of gold upon which we sit.

Division II
WHERE SHOULD WE BE?

CHAPTER 8

I Have A Dream II

"Ford got a better idea, you can get one too."

—Linda Green Beatty

"If an idea is not of your making or liking, you can choose to have a better one."

—Iyanla Vanzant

"You can't beat a thesis with an antithesis. It takes a better thesis."

—Jack Kemp

"You must not let others assign a dream to you."

—Jesse Jackson, Sr.

Martin Luther King's "I Have a Dream"[1] speech was one of the most profound of the twentieth century and easily the most important for Black Americans. Since its most prominent delivery during the 1963 March on Washington (it was delivered in other places before and after), legions, on differing sides of the civil rights movement, have taken great license in interpreting what Dr. King meant, while claiming that they are on the same page with Dr. King. My take on the dream speech follows.

First, Dr. King used the partitive article "a" rather than the definite article "the." My take from this is that Dr. King allowed for the value of the dreams of others. I believe he meant to encourage dreaming. Worthy, uplifting, ennobling, transformational dreams.

Dr. King's mastery of the language led him to choose the noun "dream" in describing his idea of America's Promised Land. "Dream" is poetic and memorable. It's parsimonious. But I interpret "dream" to be more than a dream.

In a religious setting, Dr. King might have said "I have seen a vision." A dream is differentiated from a vision in that dreams can be wild and are often unlikely if not impossible to occur. Visions are often mental images of what is very likely to occur. Visions can foreshadow what is to come. One dreams dreams, one sees visions. Dreams come while one is asleep — in a dream state. Visions can come while one is asleep or awake. Prophets see visions.

In a corporate setting, Dr. King might have said "I Have a Vision Statement" or "I Have a Strategic Plan." But Dr. King knew the expanse of his audience and the timelessness of his charge. "Dream" was the perfect word for the speech. But for those of us left to "make real" Dr. King's dream, "vision" and "strategic plans" are our tools.

> If you build castles in the air,
> Your work need not be lost:
> That is where they should be.
> Now, put foundations under them.
> —Henry David Thoreau

In this spirit, I have seen a vision. It is a vision of proportionality rather than racial color-blindness (at its most innocuous, color-blindness is a synonym for a desire to treat everyone the same. At its most virulent, color-blindness means that everyone should ascribe to middle-class White norms). Proportionality means that positive Black demographics should equal or exceed those of America's majority group and that negative Black demographics should equal but not exceed those of America's majority group. In other words, we should at least be in the ballpark of what is considered "normal" for most Americans.

My vision includes embracing our culture and heritage - our professionals, businesses, and services. In addition:

the majority of Black children will be conceived in wedlock,

the Black prison population will not exceed the Black percentage of the total population,

the distribution of school grades and standardized test scores for Black students will approximate the curve of grades for White or Asian American students.

The percentage of Black Americans in the following roles will approximate or exceed our percentage of the total American population:

elected officials from President of the U.S. to municipalities;

corporate board chairpersons, board members and CEOs;

managers;

employees;

physicians and attorneys;

scientists and professors.

Black Americans will control its demographic percentage of America's salaries and wealth. (15% of the population will equal 15 percent of the wealth)

Black Americans will own its demographic percentage of America's businesses.

On the other hand, Black Americans should represent no more than our demographic percentage of America's:

prison, jail, or corrections populations;

people in poverty;

illiterates;

individuals who are ill, including HIV, heart disease, cancer, high blood pressure, lung disease, Alzheimer's.

Our unemployment rates should be no higher than the unemployment rates of White and Asian Americans.

That's it. That's my vision.

Division III
HOW DO WE GET THERE?

Part I
LEARNING FROM OTHERS

"Strategy is better than strength."
—Hausa Legend

Other Related Models

Multi-tiered national systems are very common in America — including our form of government, which consists of local, state, and federal levels. Although the model is used by thousands of service, professional, religious and political organizations, only a few groups rely upon multi-tiered structures for their economic, political, and social survival.

Those are the organizations which interest and impress me most. Among them I count Mormons, Miami-based Cubans, and the Republic party during the Reagan years. Increasingly, American Hmongs and Hispanics are demonstrating the power of such structures. For the present, I will discuss two groups — the study of which can provide light to direct our development of a new model. One group is the American Jewish Federation, the other is the Canadian system of credit unions.

CHAPTER 9

American Jewish Federations

"There can be no collective Jewish will and vision
without a strong sense of Jewish identity, there cannot be a strong sense of Jewish identity without any
unifying corporate purpose or program.[1]"

—Dr. Gerson Cohen, Chancellor
Jewish Theological Seminary of America

Jewish federations are organizations that coordinate financial,
planning, and leadership activities among existing Jewish organizations
in an area. According to Charles Miller, former Associate Director of
the Federation of Jewish Agencies of Greater Philadelphia, Jewish Federations comprise a *worldwide service network of interrelated systems*
of local service. Federations "exist in every city of any consequence in
the United States.[2]"

Jewish Federations were conceived and founded in order to in-
terconnect members of the Jewish Diaspora who were arriving in America
from many different nations, speaking many different languages, but
still having a need to relate to one another, defend one another, and
assure progress socially, politically, educationally, and culturally. Another contributing factor was the need for collective actions on health,
welfare, and community relations issues. Overall, there was a need to
develop a sense of the caring community among Jews. As Miller put it,
"building a sense of community and developing effective means for all
elements by the community to participle is a basic motif of Federations.[3]"

Federations do not dictate to organizations how they must organize or function. Rather, federations coordinate activities among organizations.

Dr. Gerson D. Cohen, once Chancellor of the Jewish Theological Seminary of America, stated that adherence to and participation in collective action is one of the most deeply rooted principles in the Jewish historic and religious heritage, and that "...withdrawal from the community [is] a sinful abdication of responsibility."[4] Cohen stated further that Jewish identity and collective purposes are interlocked to such a degree that the two are one.[5]

Jewish federations provide the organizational structure through which the critical element of collective action can be implemented. Dr. Cohen states that "there can be no collective Jewish will and vision without a strong sense of Jewish identity, there cannot be a strong sense of Jewish identity without any unifying corporate purpose or program."[6]

In the following statement, John Gardner emphasized how critical a unifying and action-oriented Jewish structure is:

> "There is no possibility that moral, ethical, or spiritual values can be made to survive from one generation to the next if the only preservatives are words, monuments, rituals, and sacred texts. It is necessary for living men and women to recreate the values for their own time by living the faith, by caring, by doing. That is true of every political faith..."[7]

Gardner went on to say:

> "There is no merit in accepting the faith of one's fathers passively. Faith cannot be a hand-me-down. The religious, political, or social values reflected in any tradition must find new life in response to contemporary needs. This implies an active relationship to one's beliefs. What brings values alive is an attitude in the individual's commitment, a readiness to act, and a willingness to work for realization of the values. That is the heart of a living faith. The way to show reverence for values is to act on them.[8]"

In a basic way — one that relates to my proposed new model for civil rights — Jewish federations *raise money* to do what the Jewish community knows ought be done for their people. Instead of blaming, complaining to, or relying on others, through federations, Jews do what needs to be done for themselves. They, through financial security, exert significant influence on gentile legislators and power brokers to support Jewish activities.

Issues addressed by Jewish federations include the following:

Jewish identity and the Jewish family,

the elderly,

federation-synagogue relations,

Jewish education,

service to Jewish college campuses,

social justice for all people,

establishing priorities,

planning for the future.

The Council of Jewish Federations

Since each Jewish federation is a relatively local organization, local groups perceived a need to create an umbrella organization to represent all federations. The Council of Jewish Federations in North America was founded in 1932 to meet that need.

The General Assembly of the Council brings together over 3,000 Jewish leaders annually to consider new ideas, distribute materials, and share experiences. The Council of Jewish Federations has a national office and a lay and professional staff.

Since childhood, I have listened as some Black people express wonder, with both anger and envy, as to how so few Jews (Jews constitute only 2.5 percent of the American population, or approximately 5.6 million people, as opposed to approximately 30 million Black people) can have such a powerful influence on the direction of America. For example, in 2000, 11 or 11% of U. S. Senators were Jewish as compared to none who were Black. I admire the Jewish success model and choose to learn from it.

An understanding of the structure supporting Jewish activity — and the absence of a structure to support Black activities — shines a blinding light. One can like or dislike Jews or the Jewish religion. Likes or dislikes are irrelevant. It is clear to me that Jews understand the folly of being unorganized in an organized world, of being apolitical in a political arena. One can stabilize or even reverse the disadvantages of being in the numerical minority through organization and collective action.

Being unorganized or disorganized in an increasingly interconnecting world is tantamount to falling in a stomping contest, or entering a stick fight without a stick.

CHAPTER 10

The "Caisses Populaires" of Quebec, Canada

"The Caisses Populaires are not to be a charity institution, but rather a mutual assistance organization where we can put our resources together for the common benefit of all."

"What we need, next to the church tower and the parish hall, is an economic institution that will keep our money in our countryside and that will serve as a lever for our development."

"Through our savings we will attain greater dignity, a sense of duty and of the ideal that we too often lack when we are exploited. The cooperative movement shall be a school for social education and national revitalization."

"The caisses is inspired by the fertile and just philosophy of union for survival rather than struggle for survival. We wish to be at the service of our fellow man. We wish to be at the service of our survival as an endangered race."[1]

The words above are not those of Marcus Garvey, Malcolm X, Louis Farrakhan, Tony Brown, or Robert Woodson; they come from Alphonse Desjardins, founder of the credit union movement in Quebec, Canada, around the turn of the century.[2]

Among the three major financial institutions in America — banks, thrifts and credit unions — credit unions are the most user-friendly. To be a customer of a credit union is to be a voting member, thereby being a part owner of that credit union.

The credit union movement of the United States was founded by Edward Filene with the primary purpose of helping to better the lives of poor working-class employees. The credit union movement in the United States has a rich and important history, and holds great promise for the economic future of Black Americans. But this is another story.

What is more relevant to this discussion of an economic model for civil rights is Desjardins' version of credit unions or "Caisses Populaires" of Quebec, Canada. The story of the Canadian credit union movement has been explained in a videotape by Rene Caron and Marin Poire, entitled "The Unbelievable Power of Cooperation."[3]

Desjardins responded to economic conditions similar to those extant in Filene's day, but the Desjardins movement was designed for a specific group of people in a particular geographic area. As a result, there is much more of a "liberation" tone to Desjardins' pronouncements and, as Canadian laws have developed, there is significantly more power and "connectedness" in the Caisses Populaires than in American credit unions, thereby offering significantly more transferability for Black Americans.

Among the three major financial institutions in America, credit unions are the smallest in assets. To the contrary, the Caisses Populaires is the largest financial institution in Canada. Caisses ("caisse" translates into "chest" or "box" or "trunk") have more than four million members, with more than 400,000 business or trust accounts and 300,000 student members.

The structure of the Caisses Populaires consists of three levels. The first and most important level is the caisses or credit unions themselves. Groups of caisses form a federation of caisses, and all of the federations form the Confederation or the national level of the structure. Through membership in a caisse, "members can express their needs, improve their own circumstances and act on the future of the community." Unlike credit unions in the United States, each caisse is so interconnected to all of the others that the smallest caisses offers the same full range of financial services offered by the largest caisse. This is very different from small credit unions in America, which are limited to offering very basic or "plain vanilla" services.

Credit unions in the United States do share a "self help" philosophy with Canadian caisses. Both are organized to be "not for profit nor for charity, but for service." Both caisses and credit unions are designed to assist groups with something in common (a common bond), such as

56

work or community affiliation, within a "field of membership." Canadian laws are much more liberal about fields of membership; all citizens of Quebec and perhaps Canada can belong. And the interconnectedness of services means, really, one credit union for the entire nation.

Each caisse is a local autonomous organization that is run and controlled by its members, using democratic principles, with the mission of contributing to the social and economic security and freedom of its members and communities.

A federation of caisses provides regional services. It assists the government in regulating individual caisses to assure legal and ethical interactions. Canadian federations provide much more of a "policing" function with member caisses than do state credit union leagues with member credit unions in the United States.

The Confederation of the Caisses Populaires — the national organization — is a *tour de force* in the worldwide credit union movement. Through a constellation of corporations, subsidiaries, and holding companies, the Confederation offers a full range of products and services for individuals and corporations, in addition to international financial and social services. Among the products and services offered by the Caisses are:

securities and currencies;

credit cards and automatic paying services;

a complete range of insurance services, including group insurance;

trust and specialized services;

investments and retirement plans;

automobile, truck, and equipment leasing;

industrial and commercial enterprises;

venture capital for small and middle sized businesses.

In addition, there is a Historical Society, an Educational and Cultural Foundation, a Cooperative Institute (a residential teaching institute for adults); and a Society of International Development — which assists Third World nations (including ones in Africa) in developing economic and social programs of their own.

Dejardins founded the caisse movement at a time when a high percentage of Quebec citizens were in abject poverty. Banks and lenders were charging interest rates up to 3,000 percent! The majority was dirt poor, and many fled to the United States. Desjardins saw the strength in poor people learning the value of saving and grouping their meager resources to advance their own causes and to secure their own futures. In other words, Desjardins' vision was that of poor people transforming themselves from beggars and victims to being in charge of their own destinies. The vision is now reality. Les Caisses Populaires Desjardins is a model well worth the attention of Black Americans.

Part II
APPROACHING A NEW MODEL

CHAPTER 11

Criteria for a New Model: Seven Stepping Stones to a New Model

Arriving at a new model for civil rights requires the civil rights advocate to climb conceptual "steps" to approach a new model. Each step is a criterion for a new model. These seven criteria or "C's" are proffered as benchmarks whether one embraces the model soon to be presented, embraces another model, or conceives of a model. The criteria, I believe, are these:

1. Comprehensiveness;
2. Communications;
3. Cooperation;
4. Coordination;
5. Complaints management;
6. Citizenship; and
7. Courageous leadership.

Following is a fuller explanation of each criterion.

Comprehensiveness
A new model should promote *comprehensive planning*. Those plans should coordinate Black activities to address the full range of problems our people face — from education to incarceration, from Social Security to housing. The plans, models, and strategies must have importance, practicality, and opportunities for involvement for all Black people.

61

Existing plans and programs typically exclude large segments of our population. Strategies that work well in cities do not succeed in rural areas; others are directed toward professionals but not toward the uneducated. Some are intended for youth but not adults, still others require affiliation with a particular church or denomination.

We must carefully study existing and erstwhile successful, albeit limited, models — and give them credit. Rev. Leon Sullivan's Opportunities Industrialization Centers of America, Inc.; Rev. Jesse Jackson's Operation People United to Save Humanity; Robert Woodson's National Center for Neighborhood Enterprise; the self-help programs of Black Muslims; Jim Brown's "Amer-I-Can" program; and Tony Brown's "Buy Black" programs — as well as many other smaller programs that help people in areas all across the land — all must be studied, referenced, and used. Comprehensiveness means a place under the tent for all. It means closing service gaps and reducing duplication and redundancies in programs and services.

Communications

A new model must institutionalize quality communications and networking among Black individuals and groups. Goals, general plans, and strategies should be communicated to the masses.

Some communications, however, should *not* occur. During the beginning of the civil rights protests of the 1950s and 1960s, protesters sought media attention. The times have changed dramatically, yet Black people are still sharing agendas with the public. If we are to succeed in these times, some agendas should not be publicized. I say this not to support surreptitiousness. Business people do not share corporate secrets with their competitors.

Annually, national media reports are normal for NAACP and the Urban League conventions. Such sharing may be detrimental to progress. What, for instance, is known of the Mormon, Vietnamese, Jewish, or even Hispanic agendas? I have never seen a television report on the results of the annual meeting of the Jewish Confederation. As one political pundit once cautioned me, "You never write your best s[tuff] down!" "Running to the media" is a tired strategy that now hurts more than it helps.

Cooperation

The "pretend" order of the day regarding lifestyles and business management is decentralization, individuality. Futurists applaud corporations that have flexible work hours, that permit employees to work at home via telecommunications and computers.

Criteria for a New Model: Seven Stepping Stones to a New Model

I said "pretend" order of the day because power people are *not* decentralizing. And successful minority groups (such as the boards of multinational corporations) are not decentralizing. They are pretending to do so in order to continue to consolidate power and to assure their well-being.

It makes sense to organize while others are pretending to individualize. There is no way for people of color to survive by emulating the majority — to beat the larger group at its own game. At some point, one must become "centralized" to be in a position to decentralize.

Too often the modus operandi of many Black organizations in America — churches, Greek letter organizations, and professional associations — is to compete with one another. While competition is often friendly and sometimes promotes improvements in services to others, it is more often counterproductive and damaging. It emulates the worst of other cultures rather than their best, and serves as a major stumbling block to making the kinds of changes that will see all Black people improve our security and stations in life. *Internecine rivalries must be controlled.*

Coordination

Moreover, a new civil rights model should acknowledge the contributions and differences of the many Black organizations and attempt to align them around a shared vision — that of lending resources to the collective benefit of the group.

In the '60s, we argued against the concept of the American melting pot, in which all ingredients are viewed as homogenized into an amorphous glob. Rather, we argued for pluralism, for a tossed salad, in which ingredients retained their own sizes, shapes, and colors — each lending its uniqueness to a more flavorful dish — with Americanism serving as the integrating salad dressing.

In a new model, we must take our own advice. It should not be necessary for all Black people to work for Black success through just one or two "key" organizations. Contributions should be possible through any of several organizations. It should be the responsibility of a coalition structure — consisting of representatives of the other organizations — to coordinate, not homogenize, the various activities of Black groups.

For example, Black business people and Black gang members have much in common and, as a result, must meet and dialogue. Black gang members should learn to apply their considerable business skills — which include leadership, recruitment and retention, product development, marketing and distribution, human resource development, strategic planning and controlling competition — to legal ventures instead of drugs. For starters, I know where many acres of inner-city land can be purchased at a steal.

Groups should be supported in doing what they are chartered to do, what they are best at doing, what they have decided to take on as priorities. The coordination function will assure the elimination of gaps in service and that groups work with each other to provide national and international services through networks.

Complaints

There should not be any. The existing model, as it developed, made much progress. The most persistent residual has been the development of a generation of whiners — people who feel that we need to protest *all the time*. Telling other people why they owe us, how they haven't paid us, and why their actions are responsible for us being as we are worked for a long while. It is now time to move on to another strategy — a self-help strategy with few or no complaints.

Mass meetings during the civil rights movement were positive sessions. They were tension-filled, but it was an exciting tension. Participants sang, prayed, witnessed, planned, and practiced. In the face of guns, dogs, fire hoses, jail, and lynchings, people were aligned, motivated, empowered — positive. These were not bitching sessions.

The time has come to limit the time spent on complaining — the sorry hallmark of a once noble movement. The time is nigh to engage in high-level and serious social research, development, planning, and action. The time is upon us to interpolate Professor Houston's theories of social engineering into economic engineering — without complaints.

Courageous Leadership

> "It does not take a courageous dog to bark at the bones of a dead lion."
> —African Proverb

> "It is better to live one day as a lion than 100 years as a sheep."
> —Italian Proverb

Courage is a norm in the Black struggle. It has been the bulwark of our progress. And while many individuals — in unknown circumstances, in unknown places, at unknown times — have demonstrated courage in great and small ways, the critical need is for more courage among Black "leaders." Courage in Black leadership is a critical element sorely lacking today.

Criteria for a New Model: Seven Stepping Stones to a New Model

I have four things to say about the lack of courageous leadership:

1. The leadership numbers among Black people are inflated.

2. Black leadership, historically, has been concentrated on one person.

3. Recent Black leadership has not established new directions that are effective and appropriate.

4. Black America has not yet realized the need for leadership in developing a viable system of action.

The leadership numbers among Black people are inflated. The problem is a negative result of the 1960s civil rights movement for two reasons. First, when the federal dollars started flowing immediately after the signing of the 1964 Civil Rights Act, suddenly, there were greater needs for leaders than there were people to fill them. The demands were so great that new people emerged to lead — some by request, some as opportunists. Thus the number of "leaders" in the Black community inflated as former followers found themselves leading, sometimes heading multi-million-dollar agencies. Later, as a result of the Nixon policy of "benign neglect," the money began to dry up.

Then, the Peter Principle kicked in for the remaining civil rights positions. My experience has been that the least competent are the most tenacious in holding on to unearned positions. And while the percentage of poor leaders among Black people is certainly no higher than it is among White people or other groups, we can least afford the damage done by incompetent leadership. A new model *must* effectively address this concern.

Desegregation created a "brain drain." After the walls of segregation in higher education came tumbling down, many Black people who might have dedicated their considerable talents to Black civil rights were attracted to a variety of other fields. Before desegregation, the civil rights movement enjoyed an enriched pool of leadership because talent was concentrated into a limited number of roles, most of which were people-intensive, such as preaching to or teaching Black people. As a result of this exposure to the Black public, gifted Black leaders were compelled to focus on civil rights.

Civil rights breakthroughs in higher education permitted many of our brightest and best minds to find their niches in a broad spectrum of fields previously denied to them. An unfortunate result has been physical, social, and intellectual distancing between the Black middle class and the Black masses in our ongoing struggle for justice. This created a massive void between our behemoth needs and our gargantuan talents. A new model must bridge the gap.

Black leadership, historically, has been concentrated in one or a few people. We respond well to charismatic leadership. Like others, we are stimulated by powerful speakers and initiators of bold actions. Unlike other groups, we have been blessed with an abundance of such charismatic leaders.

It is in this area that we must make a sweeping change. We should have learned from the murders of Malcolm X and Dr. King that it is foolhardy to permit the leadership of our movements to be vulnerable to a murderer's bullet. A single death — be it natural or from acts of lunacy or hate — should *NOT* cause international disarray, cause the burning of cities, or jeopardize the future of coming generations. A new model must eliminate such vulnerability.

Succession planning has been a major concern in the private sector for years. It must become a major civil rights issue. Recent Black leadership has not established new directions that are effective and appropriate. Black leaders fixate on the strategies Dr. King employed in his life. Some even emulate Dr. King's mannerisms and speech pattern. By mimicking Dr. King, we mock his memory instead of advancing his cause.

We will be most like Dr. King by doing in these times what he did in his time — develop unique, appropriate, timely, peaceful, and effective strategies to solve the unique social problems that face us. Black people, as well as Dr. King's legacy, will be better served by developing new directions than by marching again from Selma to Montgomery or on Washington.

Black America has not yet realized the need for leadership in developing a viable system of action. It is increasingly clear that a mediocre system is far better than good intentions in achieving long-range group goals. Black people must translate years of talk into systems of transforming actions.

No large group — be it a religious denomination, an institution, a governmental agency, or an ethnic group — can achieve long-range goals (of security, growth, propaganda, aggression, dominance, competition, or racism) without organization through leadership. An appreciable number of group members must direct their mental, psychic, and spiritual energies to leadership matters: thinking, networking, strategizing, planning, communicating, implementing, assessing, and replanning.

Citizenship

We are required to exceed the minimum standards of citizenship — including but not being limited to supporting, rearing and educating our children; doing a day's work for a day's pay; voting and paying our taxes.

Moreover, we must give more to all members of our communities for three very good reasons. The first is that we are major recipients of the charity of others — be it the Red Cross, Goodwill Industries, United Way agencies, community foundations, service organizations or scholarship funds — Second, giving elevates others' perceptions of us. Significantly increased giving makes great strides in eradicating the perception of Black people as beggars, thieves, malingerers, habitués, ingrates, and reapers who have not sown. Third, and most importantly, there are rules that govern the spiritual universe. One of those immutable rules is this — one receives in proportion to what one gives. To receive more requires giving more.

CHAPTER 12

A Framework for a New Model

Objective thinkers join racists in asking such questions as the following:

why can't Black people stop Black-on-Black crime and murder in their own neighborhoods?

why can't Black people stop their own people from having so many unwanted, uncared-for babies?

why can't Black people keep their kids in school and make them behave themselves and learn more?

why do so many Black people spend so much time blaming white people for their problems?

Well, I hold that there is but a single answer to all of these questions and many more like them — *we have no structure in place through which to respond to the ever-increasing needs of our people, no structure through which civic-minded Blacks and others of goodwill can help brothers and sisters trapped in geographical statistical tracts in which rotten outcomes multiply.* Without an effective structure, it is virtually impossible to change norms across a large, widely geographically dispersed group which is characterized by countless internal differences. At present, Black Americans have no such structure.

Our last functional structure was the legislative-protest model. But we bartered its effectiveness in exchange for the 1964 Civil Rights Act. It was an anti-structure structure. We formed our passive-resistant, nonviolent civil rights movement to reverse the racist Jim Crow laws that developed during Reconstruction. They were laws designed to restore power to Southern Whites after the abolition of slavery.

The so-called "separate but equal" doctrine of the Jim Crow era was the *de facto* complement to the *de jure* racism of the slavery era. The structure of the Jim Crow era was the 20th century replica of the "big White house/outhouse" model of slavery — as depicted in Illustration 6.

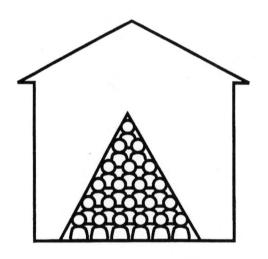

Jim Crow

Illustration 6

The structure — designed to separate White from Black — continually reinforced the notion, "If you're White, you're right. If you're Black, get back!", and increasingly "If you're brown, stick around!"

Dr. King's dream best explained the replacement of that structure. He dreamed of a single "integrated" structure, one in which people would be judged by the content of their character, not by the color of their skin.

The Dream

Illustration 7

This integration dream was scary to White racists. Their nightmares conjured up structures that caused them to redouble their efforts at separatism. Nightmare No. 1 is that of a Black takeover — the old, "Give 'em an inch, they'll take a mile" fear.

Nightmare No. 1: Takeover

Illustration 8

Nightmare No. 2 is that of "miscegenation," or race mixing. The Second Law of Nature, survival of the species, stimulated the latent fear inherent in many White people, the carriers of the most recessive of visible human genes: light-colored skin, eyes, and hair. This nightmare envisions millions of "beige" people replacing White people.

Nightmare No. 2: Beige

Illustration 9

Nightmare No. 3 was that of communism. The 1950s and 1960s marked both the height of the civil rights movement and the height of the fear of communism in America. The fact that many socialists were involved in the civil rights movement did little to quell the fears of racists who believed that the real civil rights agenda was a communist takeover of the American government. Racists, through this nightmare, envisioned the American political and economic hierarchies being flattened into a Marxist/Leninist structure of the *lumpen proletariat*. It didn't help that some outspoken civil rights activists of the time were Black artists who found more equality and acceptance in socialist countries than in America.

Nightmare No. 3: Communism

Illustration 10

Nightmare No. 4 was that of anarchy. Related to Nightmare No. 3, Nightmare No. 4 predicted that, if Black people were granted full civil rights, the American form of government would collapse. The following two stereotypes supported the nightmare:

1. Black people were too stupid to vote responsibly, let alone to be responsible, contributing citizens;
2. Communists and socialists in the civil rights movement were using Black radicals to attempt an overthrow of the American government.

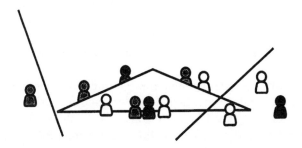

Nightmare No. 4: Anarchy

Illustration 11

While none of the nightmares of racists have come true in the nearly 50 years since *Brown v. Topeka Board of Education*, or since the nearly 40 years since the signing of the 1964 Civil Rights Act, the dream of the integrated society has not come true either. I believe that Illustration 12 comes close to defining reality for Black Americans.

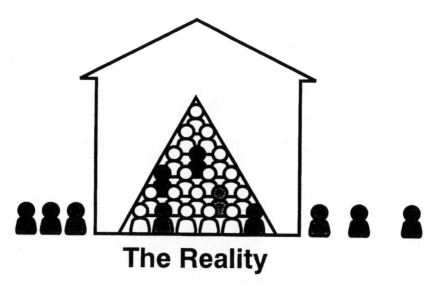

The Reality

Illustration 12

While *some* Black Americans have been absorbed into various economic and social levels, a significant and increasing percentage lives outside any semblance of organized or even civilized society. With high levels of homelessness, drug use, AIDS, murder, and illiteracy, the larger society is compelled to pay attention to the needs and pleas of the disenfranchised — those "out" group members whom most would choose to ignore.

I am firmly convinced that these intractable problems result directly from the absence of a structure designed to produce better. An erstwhile oppressed, then liberated, Diaspora should never be without a structure for securing its own peaceful, lawful economic security. Such a structure, however loosely knit and informal, should exist if for no other reason than to facilitate group communication and connectedness. It can remind successive generations of the group's accomplishments, noble purposes, and higher calls to serve humanity.

Dr. King's dream of a character-based society should be facilitated by an interconnected Black-run structure, which would make it possible to focus on esoteric group issues — be they education, incarceration, health, employment, economic development, or others. Illustration No. 13 depicts an integrated American structure — Dr. King's dream — supplemented by a Black economic substructure.

A New Model

Illustration 13

The substructure represents Black people circling their economic wagons around Black-run enterprises. The dotted line indicates the ability of Black people to move back and forth between the American economic mainstream and the Black-run economic structure. In contrast, today's Black gangs also represent an economic structure, but the opening in the wall between Black gangs and the mainstream economic structure is but a crawl space; gang members crawl through and sell drugs as they prey on the public, and law enforcement agents slip through as they pursue gang members.

Some might argue that such a substructure is separatist. I hold that many such substructures are already attached to the larger American structure, as depicted in Illustration 14.

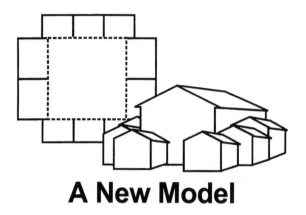

A New Model

Illustration 14

Some substructures are ethnically based, such as Irish, Italian, Native American, East Indian, West Indian, Indo-Chinese, and Cuban enclaves. Some are religiously based, such as Jews and born-again Fundamentalist organizations. Some are politically based, such as The Christian Coalition which was inspired by The Rainbow Coalition and pre-dated by the organizers of the Reagan Revolution, who developed a massive, interconnected, computerized base of supporters and contributors.

Other such substructures are emerging. Hispanic Americans have their own Chamber of Commerce and have surpassed Black Americans in business start-ups. Hmong Americans are attempting to organize a group-wide credit union. Native Americans are increasingly exercising their sovereign gaming rights to capitalize on the insatiable gambling habits of other Americans. Perhaps the only things these groups have in common are that they are all Americans, and they have developed economic structures to preserve their own identities and secure their own futures.

As seen through the lenses of the civil rights movement, the social structure of America has only two options — segregated or integrated. Professor Max Goodson[1] proffered a theory of "polarization for re-integration." Goodson envisioned the ability of a group to "caucus" on issues unique to itself without being viewed as separatist. The ability to caucus is similar to the right reserved by a family to have its own values and norms, while integrating with the larger community for work and schooling. The ability to call "family meetings" gives family members healthy and empowering means to communicate about their uniqueness — their history, noble goals, shared visions and threats, and the need to support institutions that promote their well-being.

A Framework for a New Model

Wealthy Americans have such enclaves and engage in such economic caucusing regularly. For the most part, wealthy Americans do business with a limited number of companies and individuals. Usually, the wealthy have common bonds with the owners of businesses they deal with often, a quid pro quo relationship. Those bonds can be the result of shared fraternity, religion, social set, leisure activities, charities, and communities. They tend to operate from Rolodexes, not the Yellow Pages. Keeping this in mind, I contend that economic substructures are not unique.

Dr. W. Edwards Deming said that 85 percent of problems lie within the system. I say that 65 percent of Black problems can be traced to the absence of a new model for producing economic independence.

Part III
A NEW MODEL

CHAPTER 13

A NEW MODEL FOR BLACK CIVIL RIGHTS

"Our nettlesome task is to discover how to organize our strength into compelling power."

—Rev. Dr. Martin Luther King, Jr.

"I don't like money actually, but it quiets my nerves."

—Joe Louis

"Now it was 1933, and Papa was again in Louisiana laying track. I asked him... why the land was so important. He... said in his quiet way: Look out there, Cassie girl. All that belongs to you. You ain't never had to live on nobody's place but your own and long as I live, and the family survives, you'll never have to. That's important. You may not understand that now, but one day you will. Then you'll see."[1]

—Mildred D. Taylor
Roll of Thunder, Hear My Cry

...But times have changed and it's no longer strange
    to make a few corrections in our direction.
'Cause being strong is more than just holdin' on
'Cause to advance you gotta take a chance...
What my life really means is that the songs that I
    sing
Are just pieces of a dream that I've been building.
We can make a stand, and here, I'm reaching out

my *hand*
Cause I know damn well we can if we are willing.[2]

Gil Scott Heron

Well they passed a law in '64
To give those who ain't got a little more
But it only goes so far...
That's just the way it is
Some things will never change...
But don't you believe them.[3]

Bruce Hornsby

I have a dream. The dream is one of equality of
opportunity, of privilege and property widely dis-
tributed; a dream of a land where men will not take
necessities from the many to give luxuries to the
few; . . . a dream of a place where all our gifts and
resources are held not for ourselves alone but as instruments of service for the rest of humanity...

—Martin Luther King, Jr.

I have
never been contained
Except I
made
the prison

—Mari Evans

Mama may have, Papa may have,
But God bless the child that's got his own.

—Billie Holiday

If the reader has at all bought into the notion that a new model
for civil rights is needed, then my central purpose for this book has been
met. Yet, I would be remiss were I to make the case for a new model and
then pass on the opportunity to describe a new model plan that integrates
the points and restraints I have defined. Such a model, based on economics, holds the promise of remaining viable deep into the 21st century.

Before I go further, I must re-address the existing civil rights
model — the legislative route for Black freedom. I know, as did Professor Charles Houston, that without the laws which restrain racists there
would be few opportunities for economic growth. I know that we must
be ever-vigilant in monitoring legislative processes to determine their
effects on Black people. I know that we cannot permit the interests of
others to have negative impacts on Black people. I know that the records

of those who campaign for legislative and judicial positions have much to do with the letter and spirit of laws they produce and interpret. So for the record, please know that I am for vigorous support of Black legal activities.

I believe, nonetheless, that the other peaceful route to civil rights, economic development that is, must be cleared, developed, and traveled upon regularly. We must have a balanced, two-pronged approach.

To follow is my description of a new civil rights model or plan. It is one, I believe, that can meet the criteria which I have set forth in this book.

A General Description

I propose the establishment of a four-tiered, loosely structured organization, with each tier consisting of a board of economic development. The four tiers or levels of economic development are: local, regional, national, and international.

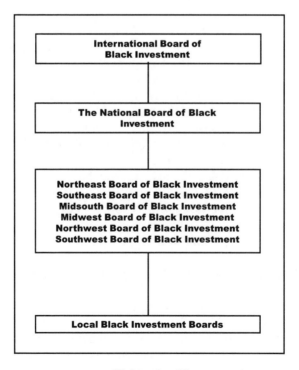

Illustration 15

Each board will consist of a panel of policymakers with a background in the financial dimension of a wide range of areas, including but not limited to civil rights, law, education, business, the arts, medicine, construction, labor relations, religion, and technology. The overall responsibility of each board will be to guide the economic development of Black people within its domain by determining and addressing present and future needs and priorities.

A board member's primary responsibility will be to assist in making investment decisions in a variety of aspects of Black life — to create the financial vehicles for pooling and investing money to achieve goals.

Local Boards

The purpose of each local board will be to receive income from local pledges, tithes, donations, contributions, inheritances, and investments. Local boards will then make decisions on business proposals — ones that they create and ones submitted by for-profit and non-profit organizations.

I propose the establishment of as many local boards as will be necessary, but each local board must accumulate a base of $50 million in assets to remain operational. This minimum asset threshold will assure that each board can make a serious and substantial local impact on the conditions of Black people within the board's geographic area. A significant asset threshold will help ensure that board members will be skilled and expert. Reasonable investors will not leave the management of $50 million to unskilled, unqualified people — something that has happened too often in Black civil rights organizations and Black churches.

While the threshold seems a formidable sum, within any sizeable city exist banks, thrifts, credit unions, insurance companies, foundations and other corporations with assets far in excess of $50 million.

The National Board

The National Board of African American Investment will be comprised of a significant number of Black persons of national stature. A representative of each regional board will also serve on the national board.

The purpose of this board will be to determine economic policies for Black people throughout the United States. It would attend to our collective economic welfare and use our collective economic strength to insure the life standards sought by most Americans:

quality education for our children,

jobs for those who can work,

work advancement,

business growth through entrepreneurial ventures and expansion of existing firms,

ownership of sports teams and previously non-Black owned firms,

social security, housing, food and medical attention for our elderly and disabled,

hope.

Regional Boards

Six regional boards will be established. Each regional board will provide services to the local boards in its region and will serve as the conduit for information and services between local boards and the national board. The set of six regional boards will be interconnected and will work cooperatively with one another.

I propose the following regional boards:

- Northeast Board of Black Investment
- Southeast Board of Black Investment
- Midsouth Board of Black Investment
- Midwest Board of Black Investment
- Northwest Board of Black Investment
- Southwest Board of Black Investment

The primary purposes of regional boards include:

1) certifying local board members;
2) facilitating communications between local boards and the National Board;
3) assisting local boards in meeting accounting and investment standards.

The International Board

The International Board, to be named **The International Board of Investment in the African Diaspora**, will be comprised of representatives from the National Board and other such boards in nations with significant Black populations. Their purpose would be obvious: to apply economic leverage in order to solve problems that plague Black people worldwide. Those problems include:

eliminating oppression, hunger, illiteracy, oppression, AIDS and other sexually transmitted diseases;

improving the public image of Black people worldwide;

assisting in the establishment of self-rule and Black economic development on island nations;

investing in the development of Black owned oil, timber, water and mineral resources;

cross-national sharing of human resource expertise and development.

The International Board will become for the African Diaspora what the State of Israel is for the Jewish Diaspora — our external mediator for international affairs. It would be a group so rich in resources that governments would be compelled to pay attention when called upon.

Criteria for Board Members

Some of the toughest decisions to be made will be those of determining who would serve on boards — or more truthfully, who would *not* serve. This is a matter I have yet to resolve to my own satisfaction. I do know, borrowing from democratic governments, that a sufficient number of checks and balances should be in place in order to minimize questionable practices that skeptics will assume to be pervasive.

Ethically, all board members should be beyond reproach. Their histories should reflect life-long advocacy for Black civil rights with no hints of fiduciary improprieties in their management of other people's money. Board members should be persons who are willing to check their egos at the door.

Regional members should be persons in the region who meet the aforementioned criteria and in whom many people have faith. They should be well prepared educationally and experientially.

National members should be of national stature. Black people should, for the most part, know them and trust them. Their backgrounds should reflect the importance of their positions. There should be consensus on their appointments. For Black Americans, this board will be the most critical in the short run. (In the long run, the International Board may be of the greatest importance.)

A New Model For Black Civil Rights

International board members should be versed in multinational finance or economics, sociology or law. They should have traveled extensively and have global perspectives. To the extent possible, they should be bilingual or better, multilingual.

Members of the National Board

In spite of significant cynicism about leadership, I would wager that, if pressed, most Black Americans could generate a list of Black people of national stature whom they trust with directing the activities of Black America and our money. I would also wager that there would be significant agreement on some names.

For the sakes of discussion and initiation, I propose the following incomplete list:

Henry Aaron	Baseball homerun king and manager
Claud Anderson	Author, Black think tank director
Maya Angelou	Poet, author, director
Harry Belafonte	Entertainer, civil rights activist
Lerone Bennett	Historian, author
Ed Bradley	Tv Journalist
Jim Brown	Former NFL star, Pres. Amer-I-Can
Johnetta Cole	Professor and former college president
Sean Combs	Music producer
John Conyers	Congress member, MI
Bill Cosby	Entertainer, media executive
Camille Cosby	Educator, philanthropist
Ossie Davis	Actor, civil rights activist
Ruby Dee	Actor, civil rights activist
Floyd Flake	Former congressman, NY, pastor
George Foreman	Former heavyweight champion, entrepreneur
George Fraser	Author, speaker
Earl Graves	Publisher, Black Enterprise magazine
William Gray	CEO United Negro College Fund
Alexis Herman	Former Secretary, U. S. Department of Labor
Ben Hooks	Past President, NAACP
Jesse Jackson, Jr.	Congressman
Sheila Jackson Lee	Congresswoman, TX
T. D. Jakes	Minister, author
Mae Jemison	Former astronaut
Ervin "Magic" Johnson	Former NBA star and entrepreneur
John Johnson	Publisher, Ebony & Jet magazines

85

Robert Johnson	Entrepreneur
Michael Jordan	Former NBA star and business executive
Tom Joyner	Radio Broadcaster
Dennis Kimbro	Professor, author
Jawanza Kunjufu	Author, publisher
Queen Latifah	Actor, talk show host, rap artist
Terry Lewis	Music producer
Julienne Malveaux	News commentator
Wynton Marsalis	Musician
Lorraine Monroe	Educator, lecturer
Toni Morrison	Author
Clarence Page	Columnist
Gary Peyton	NBA star, community activist
Colin Powell	U.S. Secretary of State
Frederick K. C. Price	Minister
Franklin Raines	Former U.S. Director OMB, CEO FNMA
Charles Rangel	Congress member, NY
William Raspberry	Columnist
Oscar Robertson	Former NBA star
Chris Rock	Comedian, actor
David Satcher	U. S. Surgeon General
Barbara Sizemore	Educator
Tavis Smiley	Radio Commentator
Brooke Stephens	Author, money manager
Susan L. Taylor	Publisher, Essence magazine
Iyanla Vanzant	Author, speaker
Maxine Waters	Congresswoman, CA
Cornell West	Professor, author
Roger Wilkins	Professor, author
Oprah Winfrey	Talk show host, media owner
Stevie Wonder	Entertainer, musician, civil rights activist
Robert Woodson	Dir. National Center for Neighborhood Enterprise
Marian-Wright Edelmann	Children's rights activist
Andrew Young	Former U.N. Ambassador

This list is not cast in stone. As I have not discussed this plan with any of these individuals, I have no idea how they would react to my ideas. Nonetheless, the list provides but a sample of the number of serious brothers and sisters who might be recruited to lend their expertise and passion to advance our ethnic group.

Board Fundraising

Local boards should promote the founding of Black-owned and Black-controlled financial institutions, with specified percentages of the annual profits of such organizations being returned to boards and/or to individual investors.

Investments from Black Organizations

Existing organizations — such as churches, colleges, and businesses — should be encouraged to invest 10 percent of their annual budgets in their local board for the advancement of the group. Specific fund-raisers, including performances by Black entertainers, could also make significant contributions. Individuals should be approached about including their regional board in their charitable donations and their wills. Investments and donations from non-Black organizations and individuals would be welcomed.

Work on King Day

Americans, especially Black Americans, have come to believe that we honor the memory of Rev. Dr. Martin Luther King, Jr. by enjoying a holiday. The irony is that Dr. King was not a "stay-at-home" person. A key word in Dr. King's life was "movement." In 1998, Rev. Jesse Jackson described Dr. King's activities on the observance of his last birthday. According to Jackson, Dr. King spent the day planning the civil rights movement's next major demonstration. Jackson stated that had someone not brought in a cake, Dr. King would have forgotten that it was his birthday.

I do not argue with the value of spending King Day studying the life and works of Dr. King, singing civil rights songs, viewing plays and art, dialoguing. All such activities have occurred continually since the assassination of Dr. King, and none of them have moved the dime.

I propose that all Black Americans and people of like-minded goodwill work on King Day and donate one day's pay or more to the National Board, to assist in funding Dr. King's dream. Personally, I feel that the same should be done on the birthday of Charles Hamilton Houston (September 3). Sacrificial work that can contribute greatly to the advancement of nonviolent civil rights is a much more appropriate tribute to the life of Dr. King than inactivity or a day of vacation.

One Year Moratorium on Conventions

Black conventions are big business. Due to cultural preferences, our conferences tend to be held in cities rather than at resorts. As a result and, again, due to cultural preferences, accommodations, attire, tours, and entertainment are significantly more expensive than they would be at a resort. These preferences cause our conventions to be very expensive.

In addition, typical of most conventions, when all is said and done, much more will have been said than done. Conventions are more of a luxury rather than they are a necessity. In many ways, they are a vacation at company expense.

As a result, I propose a one-year moratorium on Black conventions. The time void should be filled with reflection and planning, and, if necessary, teleconferences. The money saved, both by organizations and individuals, should be invested in the national and local boards. In addition, efforts should be made to measure the financial impact of the moratorium on the economy of convention cities.

Mortgage Banking and Check Cashing

Two relatively low risk and lucrative areas of finance include mortgage refinancing and check cashing operations. The primary asset for most families is their home. A focus on refinancing will reduce the risks and complexities of initial mortgage financing.

In addition, many Black Americans need to cash checks but do not have accounts in traditional financial institutions like banks. As a result, check cashing operations have become a part of the urban landscape. Most of these operations charge exorbitant fees for their services. Reduced fees can provide value to those in need of check cashing services and accrue profits for those providing the service.

Significant opportunities exist for Black America as a whole to benefit from the interest paid on mortgages and from check cashing fees. Both services offer sound and relatively low risk opportunities to accumulate long-term assets to underwrite a better future for Black America.

Black Foundation Grantee

Become the primary grant recipient of Black-based foundations.

Sample Model Conclusions

The preceding model is called a "sample" because I am not so presumptuous as to conclude that my model is the *only* one with potential. Still, I am convinced that the existence of a flexible, comprehensive organizational structure is imperative for Black people to hold any hope of improving our conditions, for ourselves and for our progeny.

Among the elements of change, two points are absolutely necessary:

1. establishing comprehensive directions, including all important phases of life and living;
2. pooling resources to apply to the implementation of those directions.

Whether it be my proposed model or some other, the challenge is the same, to return to Black people a sense of direction, of social progress through economic progress; positive images for ourselves and from others; pride in our collective and individual Blackness; and hope for our children.

A Brainstorm of Board Tasks

If board members of the caliber I have described are recruited, my thoughts on board tasks should not be necessary. Yet, I have found that an initial list of thoughts as a "jump start" for the group can be helpful. So, I provide the following list of activities for consideration:

1. organize credit unions and banks;
2. certify non-Black owned businesses regarding their "Black-friendliness";
3. provide venture capital for businesses;
4. create networks of people in business to assist in expanding client-customer bases and bidding opportunities;
5. develop catalogs of goods and services to market Black goods and services;
6. provide college students with loans, guidance, internships, and apprenticeship opportunities;
7. assist in funding the campaigns of empathetic candidates;
8. found insurance companies;
9. assist youth in developing business skills in lieu of gang participation;
10. found new Black colleges in the North and West.

Starting Points

This segment is offered to simulate thinking on what might be initial projects for the National or regional boards. I will discuss two possibilities.

First, I propose that finances be pooled *to purchase or to build one first-class high-rise hotel in one major city* — a hotel with jazz lounges instead of country and western bands; one with as many basketball courts as tennis courts; one without Prell shampoo and conditioner; one without long hairs in every tub; and one with as many Black managers as Black maids.

At the end of our conventions moratorium, if but small a percentage of the 300 national Black conventions were held at our hotel, profits would be "in the black." The "spin" in terms of jobs and work for firms would have transformational effects for our economy and psyches. Profits from the first center should be used to buy or build such a center in another major urban area, and so on.

Secondly, I propose that *the national Board buy at least one major league team in each of the sports in which Black people have made others rich*. Those sports include basketball, football, and baseball.

Most of the money for these ventures should come from investments by Black professional athletes, many of whom are: angry at the lack of Black people in front offices and in coaching and managerial positions; confused as to where they can invest their salaries in order to contribute to Black people and to insure long-term growth; frustrated with how they are treated when their careers wane and end.

Team ownership will accomplish many goals, not the least of which will be increased respect for Black athletes, coaches, and Black managers. Black people will also share in the largesse their labors and names create, and gain a say at owners' meetings.

These two ideas are offered as reasonable starting points for the national board. Certainly other ideas are as equally worthy. For example, a high point for the first six months of the George Bush, Jr. administration is the return of a few hundred dollars to taxpayers, ostensibly for the dual purpose of returning a part of the federal surplus and to stimulate a sluggish economy. To be sure, some of those dollars will be dispersed by Black people across a wide array of worthy causes. Yet, had the National Board been in place at the time of the mailing of rebate checks, it would have facilitated the concentration of rebate dollars to advance our overall liberation.

The Charles Hamilton Houston Institute has been founded to advance this model of Boards of Black investment. For those interested in more information on the institute, the web address is www.charleshouston.net.

Division IV
APPLYING THE MODEL

CHAPTER 14

Relationships With the Federal Government

It will be critical for the National Board of Black Investment to establish a new relationship with the United States government, especially in creating efficiencies in distributing and evaluating federal entitlements and grants to Black Americans. The Board can be of significant help in sealing the massive leaks of money that occur between the government and the people, due, primarily, to fattening the coffers of many "nonprofit" agencies and their managers which have made handsome livings serving as intermediaries.

Also, the Board and the government can cooperate to promote effective citizenship by alleviating poverty, thereby eliminating some sources of crime, drugs, and disease. This goal can be accomplished through the Board's work in promoting self-help ownership and employment via Black businesses.

The National Board of Black Investment should have three models through which to interact with the federal government as either (1) a major contractor; (2) a Native American tribal council; or (3) an allied foreign government.

In the role of a major contractor, the Board would oversee various governmental programs involving Black people. Programs could be specific, such as ones for the Small Business Administration, or general, such as managing a variety of programs across governmental departments.

In the role of a Tribal Council, as Indian tribes relate to the Bureau of Indian Affairs, the Board could administer block grants earmarked for Black Americans. The Board would then be in a position to make decisions regarding the distribution of funds, based on the relative quality of business plans or proposals.

In the role of foreign government, the Board would model the relationship between the nation of Israel and the United States. In the manner of Israel, the Board should request, say, $50 billion in loan guarantees to fund worthwhile large and small scale business ventures.

CHAPTER 15

Education

Public Education

"This is a real demand and society is entitled to make this demand. We cannot put so many kids out — especially not so many Black kids and minority kids — out into the great world unable to function — as we've been doing for the last twenty-five years. This thing must stop! I think it can be stopped...I don't think we exploit the techniques we have. I don't think we have made sufficient demands upon people."

"We have been willing to quit on people much too early on and I think that we have had much too much feeling that if you can adjust people to the fact that they're never going to be competent, they'll be happy and that's all we're here for."

"The society is going to insist that a self-respecting educated community stop sending kids out of school who are not literate, who are not numerate, who don't understand what it means to do a day's work. There are too many of those, and that's going to have to stop!'"

—Martin Mayer

"Until the public schools shall cease to be caste schools in every part of the country, this discussion will go on."

—Frederick Douglass

Public schools, as they presently exist, are much more of an asset to White, Asian and Hispanic students than they are to Black Americans. Bloated, top heavy, and inflexible, they are agrarian and industrial wave inventions that simply cannot respond quickly or effectively to the needs of a large percentage of Black students. Our kids are relegated to lag behind on virtually every measure. And school officials are often compelled to throw up their hands because, in the context of their structure and authority, there is little else they can do.

Little has changed as and a result of the several attempts to reform and transform public education over the past twenty years, have been useless. Education has developed immunities to change. There are too many sacred cows to be worshipped in education for any profound and lasting changes to take hold.

To follow are some changes that should be made but will not be made in the typical American school:

the length of the school day;

the length of the school year;

the lock-step, group-paced nature of the curricula;

the Eurocentric nature of the curricula;

White female dominance of elementary schools;

White male dominance of administration;

male dominance of secondary schools;

male dominance of mathematics and science;

teachers' salaries based on years of experience and degrees rather than on their relative effectiveness with children;

the school's dependence on property taxes for support;

salaried teaching positions open only to state-certified education majors.

the factory-like design and scale of school buildings

the tendency to view some students as deficient or "special."

Education

The problems that plague public education generally are magnified among Black youth.

Black people have long and deep traditions in education. In the years of apartheid in the South, laws denied Black people entrance to White colleges and universities, along with entrance into most professions. The two professions with jobs for the largest numbers of Black professional aspirants were preaching to Black people and teaching other Black people. And since the pupil/teacher ratios were smaller than the minister/parishioner ratios and the pay was better, education was the field of choice for most Black college students. Thousands of southern Black people who were qualified to pursue other careers chose teaching as their careers.

That tradition, albeit changing, still exists today. There are more Black doctorates in Education than in any other field. Black people have enormous stakes in education. Listen to the words of Professor Charles Hamilton Houston, founder of the modern civil rights movement and his biographer, Dr. Genna Rae McNeil:

> "Discrimination in education is symbolic of all the more drastic discriminations which Negroes suffer in American life. And these apparent senseless discriminations in education against Negroes have a very definite objective on the part of the ruling whites to curb the young [blacks] and prepare them to accept an inferior position in American life without protest or struggle. In the United States the Negro is economically exploited, politically ignored and socially ostr[a]cized. His education reflects his condition; the discriminations practiced against him are no accident."[2]
>
> —Charles Hamilton Houston

> "Houston was persuaded that failure to eradicate inequality in the education of black youth would condemn the entire race to an inferior position within American society in perpetuity. The white man claims black slowness, backwardness, the lesser intelligence to justify "poorer teachers, wretched schools, shorter terms and an inferior type of education" for blacks, . . . but the reasons for such treatment has nothing to do with alleged black inferiority."[3]
>
> —Genna Rae McNeil

Educational systems have proven themselves to be, by and large, incapable of making any significant difference in helping Black youth to become well-centered, learned and contributing adults who embrace rather than deny their ethnicity. Too many professional people in too many school systems do not (care to) know how to help Black kids.

If professionals in education cannot make significant progress soon (and I assume they cannot), they should be condemned, not for being ineffective, but for blocking changes that hold greater potential than the status quo.

Legal tradition drives the typical strategies for change used by Black people. We appeal to White school board members and administrators, meet with them, confront them in public meetings, and present petitions. We file government complaints. Desegregation lawsuits are still being filed and settled.

Our protests aside, professionals in Education have failed Black kids. Superintendents, members of boards of education, teachers, principals, central office administrators, state superintendents, professors and employees of the U. S. Department of Education have not delivered full quality customer service to Black children, their parents or the society.

For all of its problems, education remains for Black people their best hope. Charles Houston acknowledged the fact in 1930. The fact is unchanged. In the spirit of the two-pronged Black civil rights approach, we should continue seeking legal remedies.

Illustration 15 depicts the hard educational choices faced by Black and White Americans. The illustration intersects the polar extremes for integration with those of academic achievement.

	SEGREGATED	DESEGREGATED
Low Student Achievement	**1** Separate & Unequal	Together & Unequal
High Student Achievement	Separate & Equal	**4** Together & Equal

Illustration16

98

On the horizontal axis are the polarities of student achievement. At one end is "high academic achievement" — does the school have a record of producing high academic achievement regardless of race or socio-economic status. At the other end is low academic achievement. On the vertical axis are the polarities of school integration. At one end is "integrated," at the other is "segregated."

Quadrant 4 represents integrated schools that produce high-achieving students. I am confident that Quadrant 4 represents the most desirable option for the majority of Americans. Americans would be ecstatic if our kids could go to schools in which they experience rich cultural diversity and in which they do well academically.

Quadrant 1 represents segregated schools that produce low-achieving students. Save for a small percentage of die-hard and dumb racists, I am confident that Quadrant 1 represents the least desirable option for the majority of Americans.

Between these two extremes lie two other options. One is a "segregated" school with high-achieving students. The other is an integrated school with low-achieving students. Bear in mind that an integrated school with high-achieving students is desired by most people; however, public school systems have produced pitifully few such schools. Except for impoverished rural southern districts and rust-belt major urban areas, low-achieving segregated schools do not represent the norm as they did until the 1960s.

The norm is an "integrated" school in which educators accept Black student failure as ordinary. As a result, Black parents face two apparent options. One (Upper Right Quadrant) is to permit their children to languish in academic purgatory. The other (Lower Left Quadrant) is to seek out "Afro-centric" or all-Black schools that promote academic excellence.

A new model for Black civil rights provides a new conceptual "break the mold" paradigm that has more options than does the present "in the box" thinking. To follow are some new model thoughts on public education.

First, the mere existence of an international Black economic enterprise worth *billions* would produce a "halo effect," causing the status of Black kids to rise, based on a knowledge that a mega-organization exists to protect the rights of all Black people. Next, local Black investment boards must develop an educational arm and study the economic dimensions of education. Afterward, they must act.

Local schools must be seen as economic centers that should be controlled by the groups who live in the schools' communities. Black people represent the only ethnic group in America that perceives something to be legally wrong with being in the majority! We are the only people in America who will consistently sue to have our children (mis)educated by another group — the group we charge with being institutional racists!

Schools, aside from all the romantic palaver, represent a locus of money. Schools can be a major staple in supporting predominantly Black communities.

Think of the jobs! There are jobs for administrators, curriculum developers, and teachers of all kinds, secretaries, cooks, custodians, police officers, social workers, psychologists, and aides. Look at the capital outlay! Schools mean building construction and maintenance and sub-contracts. Schools have playgrounds, athletic fields, field houses, and swimming pools; as a result, they need landscaping, plumbing, and electrical work. Schools create contracts for heating, cooling, roof, and parking lot repair. They need mud jacking, tuck pointing, asbestos removal, and legal services.

Schools purchase instructional materials, including books, computers, films, videotape equipment, projectors, slides, and cameras. They need *tons* of paper, food, plates, knives, forks, fabric, lumber, plastics, and metals. They need toilet paper, cleaning solvents of all kinds, and office equipment, instructional computers, software programs, copiers.

As all of this money changes hands, especially in neighborhoods where Black people are in the majority, we should ask the questions: "How much school money do Black people receive? How much are Black educators, contractors, suppliers, trainers, developers — Black workers — getting?" percentage-wise, I suggest, very little.

The challenge of increasing public sector business with Black people is clear. It is equally clear that marching on the school district's main office will not accrue business results. Public schools receive money based primarily on the number of kids they are projected to have in a given year. Too often, the people who make the real money from predominantly Black schools are the suppliers of goods and services. These suppliers are often White people who have their kids in private or suburban schools and who want no contact with Black children, a major source of their wealth.

Black suppliers of goods and services must be identified. Economic opportunities should be explained, not only to adults but also to Black youth, who are constantly searching for answers to the question of what they should do with their lives. As more suppliers of goods and services to schools make more school money, they can share some of the largesse with other Black people. Then the cycle completes and repeats. The less poverty-ridden the children of such suppliers are, the better they will do in school. And schools can become the answer to their own long-term problems.

Alternatives to Public Schools

Black Americans should begin to create plans for developing integrated or predominantly Black private schools. Some should be developed immediately as model centers.

I am a supporter of public education, but public school systems — and the social police that cause them to be as they are — refuse to reorder their ways of doing things, if public schools cannot convince their bigots and leeches on the Black economy to slice the economic pie more fairly, then other, more stringent nonviolent approaches should be entertained.

Politics makes strange bedfellows. The strangest and potentially most helpful for Black people are elitist White people who do not want their kids in public schools with poor kids and kids of color. Were more Black people to join forces with them to demand passage of educational voucher bills, then more private, Black-run schools could exist and operate "in the black."

There are those, both Black and White, who believe that such schools cannot be viable. (These are the same people who believe that Black people can't do anything independently!) Such people have little appreciation of what the status quo is costing Black kids, the cause of Black freedom, and the public at large. Were such people in control of Black activity 100 years ago, virtually no predominantly Black colleges would exist.

Some fear that vouchers would serve as an instrument to resegregate schools that are desegregated. Please remember this route is recommended only if efforts to reason with public school systems fail. Also, I agree with the proponents of vouchers on the idea that competition, a good old American free enterprise concept, will be good for public schools and for Black children in them.

As of now, White people, not Black ones, are the prime beneficiaries of "desegregated" public schools. They are the ones who own the book companies, the construction firms, the law firms and, yes, even the bus companies. They are the ones who run the unions. They, therefore, have the greatest vested interest in preserving schools as they currently exist. They are the ones who have more to lose than do Black people if vouchers are permitted. They are the ones who will resist losing their "sacred cow."

I must say that I have nothing but the highest regard for our older civil rights warriors who believe that school desegregation or integration as it was conceived 50 years ago is the only answer. The question is, however, "What is happening to and for Black children even in school districts that have been desegregated for many years?"

In comparison to White kids in those same districts, what are Black kids' graduation rates, drop-out rates, averages on standardized tests, suspension rates, expulsion rates, corporal punishment rates, chances of being elected a class officer, rates of admittance to the "college prep" track, inclusion in gifted and talented classes, placement in special education classes (especially "emotionally disturbed" and "mentally retarded" classes), grade averages, referrals to psychologists, guidance counselors, and social workers, school referrals to law enforcement agencies, and scheduling in "remedial" classes and alternative schools? I believe, virtually to a school district, that Black kids are on the negative end of any set of the aforementioned statistics. This is *not* integration. It is genocide. It is intolerable.

White bodies and Black bodies sharing the same physical space in no way means that "integration" is a reality. Integration cannot be defined at the intermingling of warm bodies in hallways, lunchrooms, restroom, gyms, auditoriums and playgrounds. Integration must also entail proportional representation in chemistry, physics, calculus, foreign language and advanced placement English classes. It must also entail proportional representation in honors, scholarships and talented and gifted programs.

Besides, I have known many "successful" Black kids in "integrated" schools who were simply sharp enough to develop very thick psychological shells as a coping mechanism. They smiled, lowered their heads and their ethnic sensitivities, and plowed their ways through.

Know that my preference is for true integration of public schools, but only when that integration is true and complete. Short of that, **Black people must stop the self-effacing notion that the only good education is a White-run education** and that our many well-prepared Black educators cannot run a quality school or school system.

Well-intentioned but ill-conceived desegregation suit settlements make Black kids get up too early in the morning to board cold yellow school buses to drive past neighborhood schools, to ride too long to enter outlying schools designed and operated on Euro-American ethnocentric norms and values. Many times Black kids serve as "tokens" or "special needs" students. They are the brunt of jokes. They are too often the objects of fear and pity, punished by having to miss after-school activities to again board cold yellow buses to return to their neighborhoods late into the evening. One cannot help but wonder what would happen to the grades of Black kids if the two hours spent daily on buses, in transit, were spent in study.

Vouchers represent our best opportunity to bargain for changes in public schools. They represent our opportunity to negotiate from a position of strength for more Black input into all phases of public education for the benefit of our kids. Vouchers give us economic strike power. We will be enabled to say to school boards and their suppliers of goods and services, "Make improvements for our kids or we take our business elsewhere" — the ultimate power of the consumer.

All Black Americans should support legislation that creates alternatives to public education, especially vouchers. Alternatives, healthy competition, fear of extinction, these are the ways that public schools will become motivated enough to make the dramatic and transformational changes they must make. Also know that as the United States moralizes on the human rights of people around the world this nation cannot afford a return to apartheid, educational or otherwise. It cannot permit White people and Black people again to become so isolated from each other that one group has no idea what the other group is doing or planning, as has happened in South Africa.

Everyone wants quality. Many White people have no problem integrating for quality experiences, nor do they have problems following Black leadership if that leadership creates quality. Quality education for Black students is attainable, in predominantly White schools or predominantly Black ones, if appropriate and timely strategies, economic ones, cause them to exist.

I believe that one of the early orders of business for the local and the National Board of Black investments is to make funds available for research to determine the Black educational agenda. This need not take long, given the high number of forward-thinking and excellent Black teachers, administrators, and professors of education who already know what needs to be done but who can't get school officials to act. Then the priority will be to establish alternatives to public schools, including educational academies, boot camps, boarding schools, individualized school-based, home-based, church-based, and community-based educational programs.

Things are moving too fast for the old admonishments to Black youth to be of any significance. We are in a time when a major world super-power can begin a year appearing omnipotent and impenetrable and are nonexistent before the year's end.

While we admonish our children: "Don't drop out!", "Down with dope!", "Don't make babies you can't take care of!", "Don't kill each other!", "Just say, no!", other youth are cutting their teeth in cyberspace, mastering multiple languages, multiple musical instruments, advanced mathematics and sciences.

And what might a new model direct in terms of a curriculum? What should Black kids be taught? What are the basic and elegant subjects of study to be mastered by contemporary Black youth? Consider the following:

1. **Literacy**. Bottom line. Black children, *all of them*, should be reading at or above grade level. No excuses.

2. **Standard English**. The time has long past for understanding the basics of the English language. While I understand the importance of dialects, a child should be able to translate and move from a dialect to standard English and back at will, with ease. He or she should not be inhibited by an inability to understand, use, or write in the language of success and money. Our students should be able to shift seamlessly between Ebonics and Standard English.

    Besides, an understanding of the basics of a language leads to the ability to understand the structure of other languages and the logic of other disciplines. Confusion about how the English language works will result in significant problems in understanding the structure of other languages and fields of study.

3. **Numeracy**. Black kids should be able to do mathematics commensurate with their age groups, at least through algebra — the more math, the sooner the better. Special care should be taken to teach our children to enjoy the beauty and symmetry of mathematics as early as possible to help them overcome the fear of math. This infectious fear is caught from the adults and older students in the environment who provide the excuses for why its o.k. not to learn more math — "I couldn't do it either!" Girls must receive a double dose of immunization from this disease, given the sexist and racist notions that circulate around math. Excellent math teachers, computer-based math instruction, "real life" problems, real life analogies and applications, games — all can contribute to overcoming.

4. **A money curriculum**. While money curricula are emerging in a few places, money should be demystified for Black youth as early in their lives as possible.

    Schools don't teach about money. When kids from middle and upper income families learn about money, they learn it from their parents. They observe as their parents earn, save, invest, spend, and account for it. As they grow up, they are given accounts, money, and bonds. They are instructed, tutored, and counseled. They are beneficiaries.

What poor kids learn about money is that it is what is needed to live well, that: they and their loved ones don't have much of it; that they don't have much hope of getting much of it legally; those who have it, got it by cheating and over-charging people like them; they are angry about all of the above; in too many instances, they will get money by any means necessary.

Schools can help Black youth understand money: what is it, how do you get it legally, of what good is it, how to manage it, how to account for it, how to invest it, how to work cooperatively with others in markets to maximize returns, how to keep from giving so much of ours to other groups.

5. **Black Economic Development**. Black young people must be taught the value of money, especially in the achievement of their own freedom. They must be taught, grades K-12, about the new model and how they can participate. Each elementary student should have a library card *and* a bank account.

6. **Computer Literacy**. For now and in the future, computer literacy has become tantamount to the abilities to read and write. There are data that validate a proclivity between Black children and computers. There is a significant halo effect ("I'm special because I can run a computer!"), and computers don't have attitudes, therefore they cannot discriminate.

The greatest role for computers in Black schools is that of aide, like pencils and papers. Of course, computers as a discrete course should be available for those who show interest.

7. **Euro-American History**. I realize that it is correct first to study ancient African history, then European history, and then American history . . . , but in this regard, I hold to two beliefs.

One is that the average kid doesn't want to learn that much history, the other is that our youth should understand the cultural "backdrop" for our present state of affairs.

In other words, they need answers to the following questions: "Who are these people we call "White?" "From where did they come?" "Why are they in charge of so much and we so little?" "What have they contributed to the world?" "What have they detracted from the world?" "How did 'America' come to be as it is?"

I support the teaching of a balanced, inclusive, and fair history. As a result, I believe that if Black people were in charge of this system, then it would be important to learn Black history first.

8. **Black History**. Given the aforementioned backdrop, it is appropriate to help our youth learn the following: "How did we get here?" "Why are we here?" "What was done to us?" "What was done for us?" "What have we contributed to the world?" "What have we detracted from the world?" "Why do I feel as I do?" "Why am I being treated as I am?" "What is my world view — why do I perceive life's conditions as I do?" "What am I empowered to accomplish?"

Santayana's famous statement, "Those who cannot remember the past are condemned to repeat it," is most apt here. Since the demise of the Black power movement, Black history has been relegated to cute little activities done in the month of February (Black History Month). We are raising generations of Black children with little or no understanding of their cultural roots nor their groups' contributions to the American way of life. This must be remedied.

9. **Job Training**. All Black students should have job training skills, including emphasis on:

   - Attitudes;
   - Appearance;
   - Application procedures;
   - Resume development;
   - Test taking;
   - Interview skills;
   - Job performance expectations;
   - Career ladder development;
   - Entrepreneurship;
   - Capitalization and investments.

All students should be prepared to move from school to work, and those who do not intend to pursue a bachelor's degree should have *apprenticeship* experiences.

10. **Social Literacy**. Black students should be taught to diagnose, analyze, and solve problems of the human condition.

11. **Values Translations**. Black students and White students must be

taught to respect their own cultural values, and respect the cultural values of others, as well as the skills to speak through values to others who do not share them.

12. **Foreign Languages**. It is easiest to teach a child a second or third language while he or she is learning the primary one. Elementary school, not high school, is the best brain-growth period in which to teach a second language.

13. **Health and Wellness**. The data on trends in Black health are negative. Life expectancy is down for us while White people live significantly longer on average. Most of the contributing factors can be controlled — AIDS, eating habits, dietary fats and sugars, sedentary life styles, cigarette smoking, use of illegal drugs, nonuse of seat belts, lead in paint, murders, suicides. Most of these conditions afflict us due to ignorance, carelessness, and a "live-for-today" philosophy, born of hopelessness.

Other parents are embracing behaviors which will provide their children with early advantages. While pregnant, other mothers are: increasing their folic acid intake, exercising, and reading to their fetuses and infants to promote brain development.

Our children can be taught better and, as a result, can live better lives.

Post-Secondary Education

A predictable consequence of the decline of public education for Black youth is the decline in the number of Black students in colleges, universities and technical institutions in the U.S. The relationship between what happens in public schools and post-secondary institutions is obvious.

In addition to shrinking percentages of Black students matriculating from public schools, Black students also confront problems as "minorities" on predominantly White campuses. Attrition rates are high. Black students complain of being victimized by sophisticated forms of covert racism and increasing acts of overt racism. The numbers of Black professors on such campuses are woefully low and often the Black professors who are present do not see themselves as Black, or are so senior that they see few students at all, let alone Black ones.

While I could devote much space to expanding the description of the problem, I hasten to share my proposal for change. In the spirit of a renewed model, the center of the solution to the problem is, as it has been historically, Black colleges and universities.

Black colleges are the trump card in the game of progress for Black post-secondary students. Like predominantly Catholic, Protestant denominational, women's, and Jewish colleges, Black colleges provide educational centers with a unique perspective and support to members of a group. Such perspectives and support are critical in gaining respect outside the group.

Treatment of Black students will improve when predominantly White colleges are required to compete with Black colleges for the brightest Black students, much as White universities compete with each other now for use of the best Black basketball and football players.

In order to achieve the status of a negotiator for the talents of the brightest Black students, more Black colleges must emulate the best Black colleges for quality. Julius Lester's logic for explaining the Black Power Movement in the 1960s holds true. "Two elephants can bargain with each other over who is going to have how many peanuts. But ain't no way possible for a groundhog to bargain with an elephant. He just don't have the power... and... it's time black people stopped being groundhogs.[4]"

For Black colleges and universities to avoid being the educational groundhog, I have to make an unpopular recommendation: *Some existing Black colleges should close!*

Were the scarce resources, now being dispersed to more than 100 existing institutions, channeled into fewer, better and larger ones, the predictable results will be dramatic improvements in their quality, size, endowments, and worldwide influence, particularly in the area of social and economic change for Black people. They should become centers for advancing the cause of a renewed civil rights model. These changes hold great promise for significantly increasing the number of Black students who attend Black colleges.

With the support of sympathetic and separatist Whites, our fore parents founded Black colleges in an appropriate response to previous times. Conditions then were such that:

1. Talented Black young people could not enter southern White colleges.
2. Northern White institutions that were admitting some Black students were too far away and too expensive to be practical for Black students to attend in any numbers.
3. The institutions were needed as centers of Black history, struggle, and pride.
4. Whites were financially supportive of Black institutions as appeasements for those who might otherwise demand to enter White southern institutions.

5. Black people knew that slavery was the instrument of enforced igno-
    rance and that knowledge, if not education, was and is *the* highway
    to equity, if not justice.

Our successful struggles have required that major universities,
with rich endowments and advanced technologies, open their portals to
receive our children. They have. As a result, a significant "brain drain"
has occurred, and many of our geniuses, talented philosophers, scientists, artists and musicians have moved *away* from Black schools and
into predominantly White ones — to suffer the slings and arrows of
outrageous fortunes there. Although talented Black people are found in
abundance on Black campuses, clearly much Black talent is housed in
the colleges of the elite universities of America and, rightly so as choice
was the goal of our civil rights struggles and victories. There is significant irony in the fact that the sports teams of some historically Black
colleges are frequently beaten by Black players in competing predominantly White universities, universities in which, a generation ago, Black
students could not have gained admittance.

Proximity is not now the problem it once was. Until recently,
most of Black life depended on farms. Nearby colleges minimized families' costs and allowed college students to work at home while attending
school. This closeness also made parents feel better, knowing that their
children, especially daughters, were in nearby religious and strict Black
colleges and not "gallivanting off," being tempted in some big city "way
up North!"

Additionally, political activity resulted, in part, in the formula-
tion of President Kennedy's "New Frontier" and President Johnson's
"Great Society," which began the process of sharing some of the nation's
bounty with Black colleges. So much for ancient history!

I have often reflected on the profound impact strong, well-endowed Black colleges *can and should* have on national and international issues. But the onus of change and improvement rests on us to
merge and "right size" our colleges.

Closed campuses can prove a boon to their communities. Dor-
mitories could be rented to poor Black people as apartments, chapels
and assembly halls could become churches, gymnasiums could become
restaurants and banquet facilities, etc. Other facilities should become
business centers and incubators.

To extend this point just a tad longer, if, and God only knows
how, leaders in Black denominations were to give up their turf-watching
head trips, they would implement plans suggested years ago and merge
splintered Black denominations whose theological and doctrinal differences are virtually nonexistent. Such Black mega-denominations would

make significant differences in the social equity enjoyed by us all. Politicians and financiers listen better to "big." Such mergers could facilitate the closings of several struggling Black colleges that lack the resources, both fiscal and human, to compete even with good urban high schools, let alone other quality colleges!

Some thresholds for determining whether Black colleges should remain open or close follow:

An enrollment of 2,000 students to provide a range of curricular offerings

Comfortable accreditation -- without major concerns, issues, qualifications

Two million dollars in endowment

A majority of the students and faculty are Black American -- especially of concern for state colleges.

After closing some ineffective Black colleges, and expanding and endowing remaining ones, it will at some point make sense to fund new Black colleges in geographical areas where they do not exist, including the West and the Midwest.

CHAPTER 16

The Black Hole In the Pulpit: The Case For Black Mega-Churches

The Black church remains the most significant institution within the Black community, despite her formidable challenges over time. The Black church, like all other old organizations, is facing the ultimatum — "Grow or die!" For much of the 1970s and through the 1990s, the Black church has, by acquiescence, chosen death. Prof. John Hope Franklin's erstwhile description of the NAACP is applicable to the Black church — "[It] borders on contemporary irrelevance." Although the Black church is enjoying resurgence as the result of some forward-thinking ministers and congregations (mostly in major cities), the Black church no longer holds center stage in Black communities as it did during the first 60-plus years of the 20th century.

Hoist By Our Own Petard

In many ways, the cresting of the influence of the Black church is also an indirect result of the success of the protest model for civil rights. From slavery until the signing of the 1964 Civil Rights Act, perhaps the most powerful position in the Black community was that of minister.

Prestige and visibility aside, the minister was one of the few professional positions that existed apart from economic dependence on White people. The Black minister's salary, such as it was, came from the pockets of Black parishioners.

As a result, thousands of gifted and highly intelligent Black people were attracted to the pulpit — many because of a call from God, others because they had few other options to become a professional person. The tradition of giftedness and intelligence can be assessed by the high number of ministers who were or are also national civil rights leaders, including the Reverends: Martin Luther King, Jr., Martin Luther King, Sr., Adam Clayton Powell, Jesse Jackson, Andrew Young, Ben Hooks, Ralph Abernathy, Vernon Johns, Joseph Lowery, Fred Shuttlesworth, B. J. Smith, Floyd Flake, Al Sharpton; and Ministers Malcolm X and Louis Farrakhan.

As the civil rights movement began to impact higher education admissions policies and, later, professions, Black Americans became *hoist by our own petard*. Predominantly White colleges and businesses were enriched by our presence and, as a result, our institutions suffered a brain drain. Especially negatively affected was the Black ministry.

As the panoply of professions opened up to us, the brightest had many more options than teaching and preaching. At the same time, the number of Black churches has increased, each needing a minister. Well-educated Black pastors often hold full-time managerial positions in the public or private sector. Unfortunately, as our interests have turned to other professions, lesser talented individuals have filled the breach. In many ways, there is a Black hole in the pulpit.

Less-talented preachers are often unable to inspire youth or social change. Many parody their perception of what a minister does. They lack the skills to lead, motivate, empower, educate, or preach. As a result, suffering in the Black church and community is intensified.

The solution is the same as for Black colleges — bigger is better. Black churches need to transcend the paper-thin differences that separate many of them within the same or similar denominations to create fewer Black churches, with larger memberships for each.

Doing this will provide churches with the economic bases to hire truly gifted full time ministers and to attract truly gifted individuals again to the ministry. Such churches can offer a range of services to members that small churches cannot afford — services including but not limited to religious education, personal and financial counseling, business incubators, low income housing, televised services, elder care and day care. Such mega-churches can enhance or counter the political and religious clout of well-endowed White churches in the area.

The National, regional and local boards of Black investment can provide reasonable loans to facilitate the organization and construction of such churches.

CHAPTER 17

The Criminal (In)Justice System

"Justice is often painted as having bandaged eyes. But a mask of iron, however thick, would never blind American justice when a Black man is on trial. He will find all presumptions of law and evidence against him. It is not so much the business of his enemies to prove him guilty as it is the business of himself to prove his innocence. Indeed, color is a far greater protection to the white people than anything else."

—Frederick Douglass

The criminal (in)justice system in the United States is second only to the grave as the dumping ground for the failures of social programs and the victims of social meanness. And like all dump yards, this system needs raw materials to be profitable.

There is a **prison** industry in the U.S. Any doubts about this, was dispelled when prison companies were first listed on the Dow Jones. Industrialists and investors make fortunes by providing goods and services to the various levels of the criminal justice system. The system creates jobs for lawyers, police officers, social workers, psychologists and psychiatrists, court reporters and custodians, jailers and judges, just to name a few. It also creates contracts for architects, engineers, construction companies, manufacturers of security and communications systems, furniture and uniforms, and for food wholesalers.

Books like *Search and Destroy: African American Males in the Criminal Justice System*[1] by Jerome G. Miller and *No Equal Justice: Race and Class in the American Criminal Justice System*[2] by David Cole, and articles like "The Prison Industrial Complex[3]" by Eric Schlosser provide convincing, profound and shocking evidence of the intent to capitalize from the criminal justice system's biases against Black people.

You might expect me to ask "How much of the money from the criminal justice system goes to Black people?". Although that is an excellent question (and my conclusion is precious little), an even more important concern exists: Black people are the raw materials for the prison industry. The finished product of the prison industry is the career criminal, who throughout his/her life will provide phony justification for increased funding for the prison industry, thereby increasing profits for investors and beneficiaries. The criminal justice system can thrive only with increasing numbers of people in increasing trouble with the law.

Fortunes depend on a channel of criminals. And since society blithely assumes that Black people will continually steal, assault, rape, kill, sell illegal substances, prostitute, that is perpetrate crimes at least at the rates we have in the past, then the prison industry is a secure growth industry. Particularly heartening to prison industrialists is the reality that most Black crime victimizes other Black people.

The keys to insuring the supply of Black raw material are dope and guns. Black hopelessness, combined with drugs and guns, keeps increasing numbers of Black people, particularly young ones, on the conveyor belt to prison, guaranteeing profit for others.

The process starts with unstable families and communities and is exacerbated by school officials who refuse to teach elementary kids basic skills and self-discipline. Nonetheless, young Black men in hip-hop attire are not the ones boarding transatlantic jets to swing international drug deals. Most are incapable of manufacturing toothpicks, let alone guns.

The answer lies in *draining the profit from the prison industry*. This should be an indirect action. As Black people develop a viable, economically based civil rights model, fewer will be prison fodder. This natural decline should go hand-in-glove with organized efforts to transform the criminal justice system.

The National Board should become heavily involved in the businesses that supply the prison industry. The Board should compete to keep prison-related money within the Black community — to eventually reduce the economic causes that create prisoners. Each level of government should be required to give substantial preference points to Black businesses in this regard.

This plan, along with the overall impact of the new model, will help prison officials accomplish what should be their true mission: that of working themselves out of a job, instead of planning for the kind of cancerous growth in which the parasite eventually kills the host.

The most dangerous enterprise (or animal) is a wounded one, one in danger of losing its profit margin. When more Black people find positive directions for their lives, intensive lobbying efforts will mount a backlash to change the laws, to redefine more Black people as law-breakers, harking back to times when trying to vote or wanting to sit in the front of a bus could make a Black person jailbait.

Too many individuals have a vested interest in pretending to rehabilitate, while in reality intending to incarcerate indefinitely — for the sakes of their own jobs and/or businesses. The prison industry will need close monitoring to insure that it is what it should be, an ever-declining system.

CHAPTER 18

Ain't Gon'
Study Marchin'
No More

The last word from the Million Man March (MMM) brain trust called for four million Black family members to rally in Washington in October of '96 for the Mother of All Marches. Since then, we have had the Million Woman March, and the Million Youth March. There are plans for a Million Family March. Before there is a call for a Million Pet March, let's take a minute to breathe.

This book was written as a result of an argument over the usefulness of the 1980 March on Washington. That march and argument caused me to consider the possibility that Black Americans had marched on D. C. too often, that we have substituted marching for planning, thus wasting time and talent.

I acknowledge that MMM was a coup. It exceeded expectations and represents the first time Black Americans have collectively claimed responsibility for our future since the death of Dr. King. In addition, I respect this vision of Minister Farrakhan, although other visions such as seeking separate Black controlled states and creating a third political party are highly suspect.

I did not participate in MMM because I no longer march anywhere for anyone. Been there. Did that in the South in the '60's. While I strongly support several Black causes, I march no more.

In fairness, MMM was successful as long as it lasted, as were subsequent marches. The brothers, sisters and youth were pre-sent, reverent, and disciplined. Nonetheless, we've marched enough.

Let us consider how, in spite of the successes of the marches, other strategies will be more successful and appropriate.

1. **A new model should be definitive not demonstrative**. That there are post-march questions of "What will we do next?" signals the march's failure. A quality model empowers and defines peaceful and righteous steps for individuals to take in advancing the cause. And defining those steps should be elegant. Sixty uncoordinated and some times contradictory speeches evince more smoke than light.

2. **A new model must be economically based**. We have known for years that group renewal lies in economic development, but existing civil rights organizations are committed, primarily, to bird-dogging political developments. Marches contribute little toward advancing the cause of Black economic development. The closest MMM came to hitting the mark was a statement made by Rev. Jesse Jackson, who said, in effect, "The next march may be on Wall Street." What might have been dismissed as a humorous throwaway line should have been taken seriously. In pursuit of an economic strategy, marching on Wall Street is absurd but makes more sense than marching on Washington.

3. **A new model is inclusive**. Our longing for the successes of the 1960's civil rights movement is attributable, in part, to its inclusive nature. Members of other groups who spanned continuums of political influence and wealth were welcomed to make a variety of contributions from picketing to lobbying the President. An effective new model will welcome the contributions and presence of all people dedicated to improving the lives of Black Americans.

4. **An effective model is based on strategic planning.** A survey of the masses might produce better math. Instead of grandstanding in one city, a better deployment would be to ask 1,000 people in 1,000 cities to surround the most successful local crack house to compel its inhabitants to repent, atone, shut down and get out of town before sundown. Why not ask 20,000 to march on each of the 50 state capitols on the same day? Doing so would be much cheaper and closer to the real action.

I am pleased that each march came off without a hitch. But marches add insignificant value to alleviating the problems that plague us. Those problems will be addressed through economic development as a civil rights strategy — addressing the problems of education, incarceration, employment, health care and violence through the development of a business base which promotes ownership, entrepreneurialism, philanthropy and the founding of social service institutions. Economic development calls for a transformation in thinking and leadership; neither was in evidence at any of the marches.

5. **An effective model retains most of the money generated by the movement for Black people.** Odom's Axiom No. 1 is "S/he who walks away with the cash, wins." Any model worth its salt retains the primary resource for the cause it promotes. The medium in a new model is money, not words. When leaders call for the masses to move to one city, as do the leaders of the 300 annual Black conventions, the winners are not our organizations. The winners have names like United, Delta, Hertz, Marriott, Holiday Inn, McDonalds, American Express, Marshall Fields — few of whose investors and leaders value the cause.

Counting airfare, room and food in a major city for two to three days, I project a conservative per person cost of $1,000 to attend a million person march. $1,000 times 1 million equals $1 billion received by the winners. I'm sure the winners would wish for a million somebody march each week!

Here's an idea. Each year, the National Board will found a new bank or credit union in a different region. Seed funds will come from at least one million of us opening an account with a minimum of $1,000. We will still have our money. The money will grow and our people will own a financial institution that will tangibly support our dreams and make us better. Each city we might have marched in will be better off and so will all Black people.

> "Wherever you spend your money is where you create a job. If you live in Harlem, and spend your money in Chicago, you create jobs for people in Chicago. If you are Black and the businesses are run by people who are not Black, then those people come in at 9:00 a.m.; leave at 5:00 p.m. and take the wealth to the communities in which they live."
>
> —Tony Brown

> "Do you ask what we can do? Unite and build a store of your own... Do you ask where is the money? We have spent more than enough for nonsense."
>
> —Maria W. Stewart, 1872

Division V

OVERCOMING MENTAL BARRIERS TO A NEW MODEL

CHAPTER 19

Getting Past the Past: The Power of Mental Models

Down here, Lord, waiting on you,
Down here, Lord, waiting on you,
Down here, Lord, waiting on you,
Can't do nothing 'till you come.

Black church song

"[T]he present was an egg laid by the past that had the future inside its shell."

Zora Neale Hurston

Multiply Dionte by millions, then shrink the ability of each community to respond to Dionte's needs and you begin to grasp the scale and scope of our national problem. The best anecdotal information on the Black state of the nation can be garnered by interviewing objective public servants — police officers, fire fighters, teachers, principals, emergency technicians, social workers, and the clergy. Most can tell incredibly tragic stories of abuse, violence, squalor, illness, dependence, ignorance, illiteracy, and waste of talent and life.

The predictable response to such calamities is to search for someone to blame. Typically, Black people blame White people for their real or imagined ignorance, insensitivity, meanness, benign neglect, and racism.

And a natural extension of blaming White people is to blame the White-run government, with its institutionalized racism, anti-Affirmative Action policies, color blind, *"tinkle* down/supply side" economics, and incarceration industry.

Significant blame could be ascribed to public schools, with their Eurocentric curricula, lack of sensitivity to the educational needs of Black children, and teachers and administrators who are more interested in pay than progress. White-owned media can be blamed for their incessant and magnified focus on Black crime, while downplaying and ignoring White (collar) crime.

While we are playing the blame game, why spare Black people? Why not blame the Black rich and middle classes for forgetting from whence they came and their debts to less fortunate brothers and sisters?

It also makes sense to blame the Black church for its contemporary irrelevance; for its preoccupation with new buildings, choir robes and hymn books; for overlooking real problems in communities; for permitting the serious deterioration of Black families and of the morals of Black people; for their Mercedes-driving, slick-talking preachers; and their "pie-in-the-sky; in-the-sweet-bye-and-bye" philosophies.

For those inclined to lay blame, everyone but them is to blame. Unfortunately, fault-finding is akin to wetting dark pants. You get a warm feeling, but no one else notices.

In truth, we have blamed others for the negative conditions that have vexed and damned us for centuries with little effect. No matter how real oppressive conditions may be, and no matter how persistent and well-positioned racists are, racism is a deeply embedded societal norm that is unresponsive to blame or shame. It is a waste of time to continue the finger-pointing pity party.

The locus of our problems is our operant model, what Peter Senge calls our "mental model,"[2] from our vision of ourselves, our possibilities, limitations, and of the world. The reality that most Black people believe is only one version of reality. There are other versions. We have not always looked at the world this way. Gradually, we created this mental model, this world-view. And it served us well from the 1950's until the 1980's. Now, as with most models, yesterday's solutions have become today's problems.

> People of color must make a choice: either we accept what we believe others are doing to us, or reject it and do something else.
>
> —Iyanla Vanzant

Getting Past the Past: The Power of Mental Models

A History of Black American Worldviews

One's world view or mental model will have a profound impact on one's failure or success. A group's perception of its history impacts how its members deal with challenges to the group's growth and very existence. For example, a world view of one's group as consistently and ultimately victorious contrasts significantly from a world view of one's group as consistently and ultimately victimized.

Much has been written about what others have done to Black Americans, but little attention has been paid to our internal world views throughout our history. I accept the daunting challenge of paying attention. I am not a historian, but that does not deter me from attempting to describe the mental models that preceded the one in use today.

I recognize that the following is gross oversimplification. I also acknowledge that exceptions exist to each period's model (in many ways, as was explained in the section of the Introduction on paradigms, the advocates of the minority opinion in one era are often the visionaries that predict the next era!). Nonetheless, I offer sketches of the periods, and their corresponding world views, in the lives of Black Americans to underscore the power of mental models. For each of six periods, I will explore three categories: Black self-perception, goals, and dominant strategies.

Model 1
Period: Initiation of African slavery to Pre-Civil War (circa 1619–1861)
Black self-perception: Hopeless
Goals: Survival, freedom in heaven
Dominant strategy: Pleasing White slave masters

Model 2
Period: The Civil War (1861–1865)
Black self-perception: Hopeful
Goals: Freedom on earth, survival, helping the union
Dominant strategies: Fleeing to the North, grudging compliance to slavery, joining the union army, insurrections

Model 3
Period: Reconstruction (1865–1877, ending with the withdrawal of federal troops from the South)
Black self-perception: Emerging as first-class citizens
Goals: First-class citizenship, prosperity
Dominant strategies: Establishing institutions (e.g., church denominations, colleges), becoming educated, running for political office, including Congress

Model 4

Period: Early Post-Reconstruction/Jim Crow (1877–1954, ending prior to the Supreme Court case *Brown v. Topeka, Kansas*)
Black self-perception: Hopeless
Goals: Survival, freedom
Dominant strategies: Grudging compliance, prayer

Model 5

Period: Late Jim Crow (1954–1968, ending with the death of Martin Luther King, the defeat of Hubert Humphrey, and the election of Richard Nixon as president)
Black self-perception: Aggrieved, determined, defiant
Goals: First-class citizenship, integration
Dominant strategies: Legal challenges, protests

Model 6

Period: Contemporary (circa 1968 to present)
Black self-perception: Aimless
Goals: Pursue the legal protest agenda, prosperity
Dominant strategies: Protesting real and perceived discrimination; prosperity, avoidance of controversy

Model 6, our present world view, contributes to our problems as much as does institutional White racism. Maybe more so. In other words, we are stuck. The times have marched on, but our strategies have not because our world view has not.

In the absence of effective contemporary strategies, groups and individuals tend to retreat to the familiar, to the last era of success. For most Black Americans, that was the mid-1960s. The irony is, even in the 1960s many Black people were highly critical of Rev. Dr. Martin Luther King, Jr. and of the Johnson administration, which was the administration credited with having done the most for civil rights. The idea was "the more we complain, the more resources we get." Some are never satisfied.

As a result, the White model on how to deal with Black people made a dramatic shift in the Nixon administration. It went from Affirmative Action to Daniel Patrick Moynihan's philosophy of benign neglect. Black strategies did not change to counter this shift in national policy. As a result, the Nixon strategy, aided by the death of Dr. Martin Luther King, scored big points with the majority of White Americans who felt had done enough for civil rights (even though no demonstrable improvements were evident). The civil rights community continuously missed the target.

In the next chapter, I explore how the present model came to be.

CHAPTER 20

Barrier One: "They Owe Us"

Deep in my heart, I do believe,
We shall overcome someday.

One of the greatest points of departure between White and Black Americans is whether or not White Americans owe anything to Black Americans for past discrimination. Since the election of Richard Nixon to the presidency in 1968, a majority of White Americans have been saying "We've paid enough!" while a majority of Black Americans continue to believe that America still owes us and owes us big time.

Most Black Americans do not count welfare and AFDC (Aid to Families with Dependent Children) as reparation settlements; a majority of White Americans, however, feel that reparations is exactly what those payments represented. Not only that, many White Americans believe that Affirmative Action is a form of reparation that has been paid and should be ended.

Over the years, various reparation plans have been proffered (In Chapter 28, I elaborate more fully on the Reparations Movement). They range from the bogus "40 acres and a mule" commitment made by the U.S. government to freed slaves, to the "return to Africa" movement of Marcus Garvey, to an ill-fated proposal by Minister Louis Farrakhan that the government would turn over a number of states to Black control.

While an increasing number of Black Americans hold that the issue is about equal opportunity in the present, not about reparations for the past, the current civil rights/protest model continues to promote worldwide a perception that Black Americans — all 33,000,000 of us — are walking victims, that America's racist system has caused us to be poor, pitiable, and pathetic. The belief is that America owes us and must pay up. On a recent national talk show, a Black college student told a booing audience (in effect) "You inherited the debts of your forefathers and I'm here to collect!"

In the interest of strategic planning, let us, hypothetically, look at the "America owes reparations to its Black citizens" position. "If White Americans refuse to pay or even to acknowledge the debt, what then? Should we:

- starve?
- go homeless?
- go to jail?
- become drug addicts *en masse*?
- rear generations of crack cocaine babies?
- become a permanent underclass in America?
- abuse children?
- commit Black-on-Black murders?
- sire millions of Black babies who don't know their fathers?
- leave those babies to 13-and 14-year-old child-mothers to rear alone?
- refuse to inoculate those babies from childhood diseases?
- allow children to go hungry or to suffer from poor care?
- condemn Black babies to drug addiction and AIDS infection *in utero*?
- send Black children to pre-school and kindergarten with no knowledge of the alphabet, numbers, shapes, or colors?
- send Black children to schools with no knowledge of how:

  - to sit still;
  - to follow directions;
  - to keep their hands to themselves;
  - to spell their own names?
  - allow Black boys to believe that prison is a normal part of their future?
  - become hopeless, angry, and bitter?
  - refuse to register and vote in elections?
  - abuse our own health?
  - have the highest drug addiction, heart attack, high blood pressure and AIDS infection rates in the nation?"

Do we exact revenge by creating fewer institutions, owning less land, owning fewer businesses than other groups, and having less hope than did the freed slaves?

I am reminded of the scene in Mel Brooks classic farcical western movie *Blazing Saddles.* The new Black sheriff, played by the late Cleavon Little, was surrounded by bad guys. He saw no way out. To escape, he took his left hand and grabbed himself around the throat. He pulled his six-shooter from his holster and put the gun to his own temple and said, "Drop your guns, or I'll kill this nigger!" Stunned, the bad guys dropped their guns, and the sheriff eased himself out of harm's way.

That which works well in a farce is suicidal in real life. Taking ourselves hostage until the opposition gives up is suicidal. Today's bad guys would say. "Go ahead and shoot. It will save us a bullet!" It is ultimately self-destructive to pretend to retaliate against the descendants of former slave masters by enslaving ourselves, by doing more damage to ourselves in the present than impotent, ignorant racists ever could.

Prescription for Overcoming Barrier One

If revenge is the motive for the lack of reparations payments, then our best strategy is to be successful without the repa-ration. The adage, "living well is the best revenge" is so true.

We *have* been grievously and unspeakably wronged, yet society does not owe each of us a life or a living. Society is not accountable for the opportunities we have squandered, our lack of organization, or our ineffective institutions. At some point, citizens must understand that a society cannot raise every child, and government assistance is not a reliable long-term source of income — note the elimination of welfare programs with the blessings of liberals and most Black Americans.

I am not consumed with seeking or receiving reparations, but for those who are, *reparations are most likely to come to those who are successful without them.* The best way to demand respect is by taking care of our children, obeying reasonable laws, educating ourselves, remaining hopeful and empowered, owning businesses, and networking to leverage political influence.

Other groups are asking Black America this question: "If we don't pay you more money, what will you do about it? Self destruct?" Debtors are more likely to pay their debts to people whom they respect. They are less likely to repay those whom they pity or loathe.

In his "I Have a Dream[1]" speech, Dr. King stated that America's promissory note to Black Americans had been returned stamped "Insufficient Funds." Dr. King was right. Nearly forty years later, the note remains unpaid. But paid or not, self destruction and revenge are the wrong foundations upon which to found a movement.

CHAPTER 21

Barrier Two: White Man as the Center of the Universe

"As long as the colored man look to white folks to put the crown on what he say... as long as he looks to white folks for approval... then he ain't never gonna find out who he is and what he's about."

—Ma Rainey's Black Bottom [1984], act 1

The world view of the Black protest model positions the White man at the center of the Black universe. White people are empowered to decide whether or not Black people are happy and secure, thus making the White man a god on earth.

This world view determines happiness by how liberal White people are in making up to Black people for past discrimination. The White god is a good god when:

Civil rights is a priority on the national agenda,

White people acknowledge that institutionalized racism exists,

White people confess that they have done and are doing wrong to Black people,

White people commit to make amends,

Black people receive, without interference, more and more billions of dollars from government, business, and charities.

The White god is a bad god when:

White people refuse to acknowledge their responsibility for past discrimination,

White people see racism as a personal problem of a few people,

Priorities other than civil rights hold center stage on the national agenda,

White people practice to benign or malignant neglect,

White people attack entitlement programs,

White people pay lip service, but little else, to civil rights,

Activities that counter Black civil rights emerge, such as the appointment of conservative ideologues to judgeships, the re-emergence of hate groups like the Ku Klux Klan, Skinheads, and Neo-Nazis.

The model defines but one continuum of interchange with the White power structure, and that continuum ranges from ultra-compliance (Uncle Toms) to ultra-rebellion (armed militancy). Either way, the White man is the vortex of Black ideas, interactions, and reactions.

Compliant White-people worshippers have been the subject of scorn among the masses of Black people for hundreds of years.

In truth, there are still Black Americans who, given the choice, would prefer to be White. They live their lives gaining entrée to positions based on their Blackness, only to eschew all things Black.

While it is obvious that White people are the center of the universe for Uncle Toms, it is not as obvious that the same is true for many Black militants! There are Black people who are so consumed with rage that they find it difficult to accomplish very much, based on a perception that White racism inhibits their efforts. As an acquaintance put it, "I keep one foot cocked at all times!" As the protagonist in the play *I'm Not Rappaport* declared, "The only response to the outrageous is to be outraged."

Yet, the question begs to be asked: "Why are so many Black people so angry with White people?" The embarrassingly truthful conclusion is that it is White folk worship — White man as god.

Barrier Two: White Man as the Center of the Universe

To children, the parent is god. Little kids direct anger at their parents when they don't get their way. Blaming daddy and mommy for a screwed up childhood is the staple of trash TV and legal insanity defenses.

A serious self-analysis will lead to the solid conclusion that White people have no more answers for our lives than they do for their own. Acceptance of this conclusion will assuage our anger and will empower us to seek better solutions. The secure people in America and the world realize that one need not be hostile in interacting with "undeified" others.

A world view based on our strengths, needs, and desires will mean the redirection of our psychic energies from the wastefulness of anger and constant banter with White people to positive and meaningful self-directed activities. These activities will produce, as a by-product, improved relationships.

Latter-day activities of the Ku Klux Klan are last-ditch efforts by White hate-mongers to return America to a time when White men were gods in America, not only subconsciously, but in fact. The sub-liminal power of the "White-man-as-god" syndrome is evidenced by the group of "serious" candidates that run for President of the United States every four years. The brilliant, gifted, and qualified women and people of color — who form the majority of Americans — all stand aside so that, typically, several profoundly average White men vie to join the exclusive, unbroken string of "good ole White men" who have served as President since 1789. What are the odds that all of the most qualified persons for President would come from one sex in one ethnic group?!

Extrapolate those odds to the Senate, the House of Representatives, state governorships, state legislatures, the Supreme Court, judge-ships, mayors, corporate CEOs, school superintendents, the military, college presidents, boards of directors, pastors, union leaders, middle and front-line managers of all sorts — and you begin to understand. Black people are not the only ones ascribing to the "White-man-as-god" theory.

The historic under-utilization of America's human resources is incredible.

All White men can't be that smart. All people of color and women can't be that dumb.

Prescription for Overcoming Barrier Two

An updated Black world view is overdue. White people are not gods. They do not belong at the center of any universe but their own, and we need to take them off the hook so that they are no longer cast in the difficult position of playing God.

I am reminded of the Wizard of Oz who was just an ordinary man whom others chose to deify. His ego caused him to accept their adulation and responsibility for solving everyone's problems. I am also reminded of the line in the song, "Oz never did give nothing to the Tin Man that he didn't already have."[2] It is time that both they and we start putting the true God at the center of all of our universes and begin dealing with one another as equals.

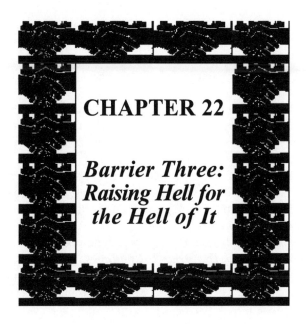

CHAPTER 22

Barrier Three: Raising Hell for the Hell of It

Protest is running amuck!

Black Americans protest against White-owned, Jewish-owned, Asian-owned, and Black-owned stores in Black neighborhoods. Many of us feel obliged to support every strike or act of civil disobedience called by every union or minority group, while those same unions and minority groups view us as so dedicated to protest that they dare to compare their plights to ours and dare to call us hypocrites if we refuse to rally on call. Some are quick to say that they are being treated like "niggers" — *the* word selected to entice the Black pit bulldog to gnaw through its chain and "sic" whomever they say.

All of this protest has caused White Americans to suffer from empathy fatigue and Black Americans to suffer from protest fatigue. Anger comprises much of our legacy. Consequently, we have reared at least two generations of Black kids who know how to do little else but protest.

While we have taught our progeny how to protest, we have not taught them:

Why they should protest (to improve their lives and the lives of other Black people);

When to protest (selectively);

How to protest (nonviolently, with moral correctness and authority, using the system against itself); and

Against whom or what to protest (the forces of racism).

As a result, we are protesting against almost everything almost all the time. We protest our housing, schools, the government, work, White people, Asian people, Hispanics, Jews, conservatives, liberals, rich people, one another, life!

To maintain a protest attitude, we must eschew reaffirming messages — messages that inspire positive attitudes and positive actions. We must believe that any Black person who is happy is either stupid or a sellout. Life must be hard.

The messages from our major organizations give no solace. The theme of the NAACP is *The Struggle Continues*. The implication is that the struggle will never end. We will never win. The theme of the United Negro College Fund is "A mind is a terrible thing to waste." Let us protest wasting a mind.

Prescription for Overcoming Barrier Three

One notion is that one's thoughts influence one's realities. Our collective focus on the negative aspects of our existence creates negative realities for us. Our focus on protest gives inertia to protest.

We must believe in and call upon the power of the God within, the power of the subconscious, the power of positive thinking, the power of faith, and the power of a reaffirming vision.

We must also "claim the victory." This strategy urges us to simply declare victory even though the battle is not yet over. Claiming victory prompts a people not to doubt the eventual outcome.

Listen to the prophetic words of Professor Charles Hamilton Houston, the father of the civil rights movement:

> "There come times when it is possible to forecast the results of a contest, of a battle, of a law-suit long before the final event has taken place.
>
> And so far as our struggle for civil rights is concerned, *the struggle for civil rights is won.*
> What I am more concerned about is the fact that the Negro shall not be content simply with demanding an equal share in the existing system.

> It seems to me that his historical challenge is to make sure that the system which shall survive in the United States of America shall be a system which guarantees justice and freedom for everyone.[1]"

Claiming victory inspires a people to behave as if winning is *fait accompli*. Doing so inspires a people to resist the temptation to view themselves as perpetual victims and losers. Doing so motivates a people to prepare for winning.

We are compelled to push protest to a back burner and to replace it with a more positive and reaffirming world view — with a model that inspires: construction over destruction; positivism over negativism; feeling good over feeling bad; security over insecurity; hope over hopelessness; life over death.

At this juncture, I introduce **Odom's Axiom Number 7**: Abandon any strategy that hurts you worse than it does your opponent. About our unyielding dedication to using protest as our primary civil rights strategy, we all would do well to heed these words of Deuteronomy 2:3: "*Ye have compassed this mountain long enough; turn ye northward.*"

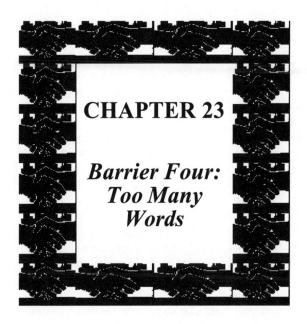

CHAPTER 23

Barrier Four: Too Many Words

"Fewness of words, greatness of deeds."
—Abdul Baha

There are too many words about what is wrong with the world, with White people, with Black people.

I recall in the 1960's when "rapping" (then it was just talk — no background music) came into vogue. People would have "rap sessions," in which most if not all participants shared their perspectives on what needed to be done — by someone else. Many people whose needs for attention far exceeded their analytical skills took center stage, with seemingly endless diatribes on a variety of topics related to "the man" and on who ought to do what. Some were intellectual diamonds in the rough, many were rocks in the rough. If the verbal flatulence could have been captured, there would never be a fuel shortage.

Not only has their legacy lived on, *they* live on — still talking, still counting the angels on pinheads, still telling tales "…full of sound and fury that signify nothing" And they have heirs — "rap music" (an oxymoron if ever I've heard one!) stars. I enjoy some rap music, but for the most part, I find most of it to be the fulminations of young Black men who have talked for many more hours than they have read.

Yet, rap stars are attempting to fill a massive void. They are trying to define a vision of the future by attempting to articulate present conditions as they know them. Black intellectuals have given us the name

"African American," but they have failed to define a viable model that makes sense to young Black people — leaving them to rap while the world trudges on.

We have arrived at a point where almost every damn body is an expert, but little improves by way of Black progress. As the quote goes, "When it's all said and done, there's much more said than done."

In the 1940's, Professor William I. deHuszar declared that America was degenerating into a "talk" democracy from having been a "do" democracy. He warned that to restore democracy, we must begin to do what we can — by active participation, working in small groups, in small ways to make a difference.[1] deHuszar felt that the best answers lie within citizens, not in Washington, DC. The time for active participation in one's own liberation, a la deHuszar, has returned.

While I concur with S. I. Hayakawa's notion that nomenclature is critical to the problem-solving process[2] words cannot alone be the medium of change. Words must be followed with actions. Field experiments, where theories are tried in the crucible of life, are equally critical. We are admonished, "By their works ye shall know them."

We must get about the business of doing — in small and large ways. Sitting on the sidelines, fussing about how awful things are, will no longer cut it.

Prescription for Barrier Three

The time has passed for Black Americans to develop a viable model for the present and future. The model presented in this book may or may not be *the* model. If this is not *the* model today, then our group needs to define or discover *the* model. Even if every Black person in America were to agree on a model, it would still take years for a noticeable change in the life conditions of the neediest among us.

As the old church song goes, "Everybody talking 'bout heaven ain't going there." The time is well nigh to not only "talk that talk," but to also "walk that talk." As the late Marvin Gaye sang, "Let's get it on!"

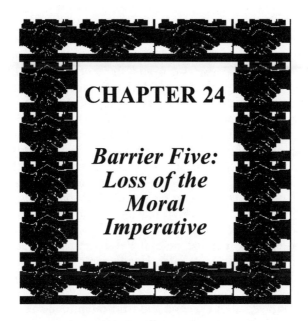

CHAPTER 24

Barrier Five: Loss of the Moral Imperative

"Let us not seek to satisfy our thirst for freedom by drinking from the cup of bitterness and hatred. We must forever conduct our struggle on the high plane of dignity and discipline. We must not allow our creative protest to degenerate into physical violence. Again and again we must rise to the majestic heights of meeting physical force with soul force."
—Rev. Dr. Martin Luther King, Jr.

The load-bearing wall for the civil rights structure was "moral correctness." When Dr. King began his leadership of the civil rights movement in Montgomery, Black people were true victims. For the most part, we were God-fearing, hard-working, patriotic citizens, oppressed by a system of legal racism and terror. We took care of our children and the children of our neighborhoods. In such an environment, Dr. King and others were able to appeal to the nation's sense of fairness, justice, ethics, godliness, and of Christianity.

The televised pictures of water hoses, dogs, night sticks, and guns turned on a nonviolent, religious people created outrage in America and the world. The moral imperative to rid the nation of legal discrimination was brought to the uninformed and uncaring in vivid black and white.

The denouement of the civil rights movement began with the emergence of the Black Power Movement from the Student Nonviolent

Coordinating Committee — an outgrowth of the Southern Christian Leadership Conference. In stark contrast with the mainstream civil rights movement, the leaders of the Black Power movement espoused a philosophy of "any means necessary" and, upon occasion, publicly brandished weapons. The young turks of the Black Power movement blurred intent, mixed messages, and bifurcated loyalties.

For all the good that the Black Power Movement did — and it did much good — its genesis also marked the unceremonious climax of the old-line civil rights movement. The old line held to the moral high ground of peaceful civil disobedience that sustained the civil rights movement for decades, and it was the moral high ground that has endeared the memory of Rev. Dr. King to the world. This loss of the moral high ground has transformed the civil rights movement from a ferocious panther to a toothless (paper) tiger.

I hasten to say that the moral imperative was a collective one. In general, we were a good, well-intentioned people. Individuals had their indiscretions, peccadillo and brushes with the law, but for the most part, we were innocent and aggrieved.

Today, we still are a good and well-intentioned people, but our tolerance of those who would give Blackness a bad name has increased to an unacceptable level. A significant percentage of young Black men and women do not operate on the ethics of the founders of the civil rights movement. The values of family, marriage, parenthood, hard work, education, lawfulness, civic responsibility, and civility are alien if not laughable in parts of the contemporary Black culture.

Institutionalized racism contributes mightily to the way things are. But never before in our history here have we been more empowered to effect our own destiny, and never before in our history have we been so confused about what we want and so inept at organizing to achieve change.

We seem unable to stop carrying the water for the "massahs" of institutionalized racism. This schism between goals and actions creates a dual personality within Black people that is projected to the public through our words and deeds. This schizophrenia is most apparent when the Ku Klux Klan emerges either in the national media or in urban areas. The fervor, the ire, the rage with which the Klan is renounced is swift, profound, and right. We should not sit dispassionately by while an organized hate group preys upon a community's fears and needs for security.

The response of Black people and Black civil rights organizations to the scourge of gangs and atrocities, however, is slow, weak, and wrong. We should not sit quietly by while organized groups prey on a community's fears and needs for security — regardless of the skin color of the people in the group. The marches, the press conferences, the chiding of police departments and other public officials, the resolutions that result from the Klan rearing its ugly head should also be the Black response to gangs' drug sales, robberies, murders, and threats.

Our unequal responses to the Klan and to gangs undermine our moral authority. Clearly, it is wrong for White people to threaten, terrorize, and kill Black people. It is equally wrong for Black people to do so, but our inaction says the opposite.

There is no question that the American system of overt and covert racism has been responsible for the deaths of tens of millions of Black people: in the holds of slave ships; in slavery; by lynchings and murders through the Jim Crow era; through the stress created by the denial of opportunities; from being compelled to live in environmentally polluted areas; from lack of access to quality medical care.

There are no hard data of how many of us have died as a result of institutionalized racism. But there are hard data on the Black-on-Black carnage being wreaked every day on the streets of America's cities. There are no excuses for the number of Black people who are murdered and injured by other Black people, and thankfully, the trends are downward.

Also, most Black people who are called "nigger!" nowadays is by another Black person. I've listened to cuts from some rap song on the radio where every other word is bleeped. And the artist is usually some young brother addressing other Black people. "Hos", bitches, m.f.'s and niggers appear to be the nouns of choice.

I must confess that I am no choir boy and have used the full range of linguistic options offered by the language. Nonetheless, constant scatological references about Black people by Black people diminishes our esteem in our own eyes and in the eyes of others.

Overcoming Barrier Five

We must regain the moral high ground in our struggle against institutionalized racism, especially in its most overt forms, as expressed by the re-emergence of the Klan. This is best done by answering the question, "Have we done everything we should have?"

We strengthen our hand in dealing with all forms of racism when we address the manifestations of hatred and terror within our group as passionately as we address the forces attacking us from the outside. Our model for civil rights must acknowledge, explain, and correct the inconsistencies in our behavior as we deal with internal and external forces that prevent the achievement of positive group goals.

CHAPTER 25

Barrier Six: Aversions to Transformation

Systems, be they organic or organizational, have built-in defense mechanisms. People and organizations instinctively resist change, yet the times require radical and sweeping change. It is happening all around us.

Of the several models of transformational change, my favorite is that of Dr. George Land, who created a paradigm having what he calls three (but what I will call four) phases.

In Phase One, the organization (division or department) is in its infancy. It is searching for meaning, direction, and market share. It suffers from many of the exigencies that befall those who are young and weak. Phase One organizations and groups require close attention and care, lest they die.

Organizations that survive Phase One move into Phase Two. Phase Two is described as the most exciting time to be in an organization. The organization is in its adolescence. It is full of vim and vigor. Its products or services are being noticed, accepted, and requested. It hires young staff. Growth rates are in double figures. Things are hot!

After a while, the organization settles down. Employees begin to fall into routine activities. The organization moves into middle age — Phase Three — and so do employees. Maintenance, not innovation, becomes the motto. Predictability, security, sameness — these are what employees appear to want. People who want innovation, change, and dynamism are quietly or openly encouraged to shut up or move out.

Employees begin to pray the Upton Prayer which goes, "Lord, let there be no major changes until after I retire."

Dr. Land believes that most American organizations are stuck in Phase Three or what he calls Late Phase Two. It does not take a genome researcher to recognize the inertia of organizations stuck on maintenance in a global market characterized by rapid transformational change.

Land states that the organizations that will survive and thrive beyond the 1990's are ones that will quickly and willingly move into Phase Four — a period of regeneration and renewal. In this period, organizations must ask themselves some basic but hard questions, including, "Who are we?" "Who are our customers?" "Who represents our competition?" "What can they do to reduce our market share, to replace us?" and "How can we do what our competition would like to do, before they do it to us?" In short, "How can we take ourselves to the next level of performance?"

Such changes are occurring and multinational conglomerates are transforming. But "What," you may ask, "does this have to do with civil rights?"

Prescription for Barrier Six

Well, major corporations need to transform themselves; so do all levels of government; so do school systems and universities; and so does the NAACP, the Urban League, Black national organizations, Black colleges, and Black churches.

Black people can no longer rely on "horse and buggy" organizations to effectively represent us in a world of Stealth aircraft. Our organizations must transform themselves to respond to current and future realities.

The hypocrisy with which Black people compel others to change while refusing to do so ourselves must end. A significant part of our children's plight results from the inaction of "fat and happy" civil rights leaders and organizations. These leaders have become secure and satisfied with old "blame and protest" strategies that pay them six-figure salaries and produce little change for the people they claim to represent.

Division VI
EPILOGUE

CHAPTER 26

2003: Jubilee II

In 1963, in front of the Lincoln Memorial in Washington, D.C., Rev. Dr. Martin Luther King, Jr. shared his dream — a vision of the Promised Land for people of color in the United States of America. Like Moses, Dr. King came to realize that "I may not get there with you..."

Martin, like Moses, led his people to the edge of the Promised Land. Martin, like Moses, was allowed to look over into the Promised Land but not to enter it. Moses and Martin told us "what" to do — enter the Promised Land — but it was not their responsibility to tell us "how" to do it.

For the ancient Israelites, that job fell to Joshua. For Black people today, **we** are Joshua.

When the Israelites lost faith and refused to enter the Promised Land and fight, God caused them to languish in the desert for 40 years — for those without faith to die. In the 40th year, the children of Israel entered the Promised Land, fought and prevailed.

The word "jubilee" has special historical significance to Black Americans, especially with the ancient Jewish religious experience from which the word originates. Webster's New World College Dictionary* defines "jubilee" as *Jewish History a year-long celebration held every fifty years in which all bondmen were freed, mortgaged lands were restored to the original owners... an anniversary, esp. a 50th or 25th anniversary... a time or occasion of rejoicing.*

The year 2003 will be the 40th anniversary of the 1963 "I Have a Dream" speech. We should proclaim it as the year in which Black Americans will celebrate the beginning of our ultimate jubilee — that of economic equity and legal equity.

> *"God changeth not what is in a people until they change what is in themselves."*
> —Koran

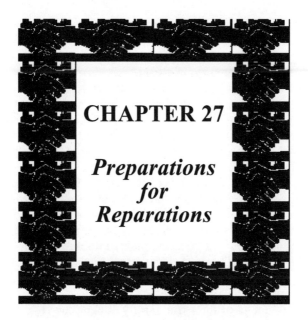

CHAPTER 27

Preparations for Reparations

"Go where you may, search where you will, roam through all the monarchies and despotisms of the Old World, travel through South America, search out every abuse and where you have found the last, lay your facts by the side of the every-day practices of this nation, and you will say with me that, for revolting barbarity and shameless hypocrisy, America reigns without a rival."

—Frederick Douglass

"By the rivers of Babylon, there we sat down, yea, we wept, when we remembered Zion. We hanged our harps upon the willows in the midst thereof. For there they that carried us away captive required of us a song; and they that wasted us required of us mirth, saying, Sing us one of the songs of Zion. How shall we sing the Lord's song in a strange land? If I forget thee, O Jerusalem, let my right hand forget her cunning. If I do not remember thee, let my tongue cleave to the roof of my mouth..."

—Psalm 137:1–8

"Southern trees bear a strange fruit
Blood on the leaves and blood on the root
Black bodies swinging in the Southern breeze
Strange fruit hanging from the poplar trees."

—Lewis Anderson
as sung by Billie Holiday

149

Upon hearing about the movement for reparations for Black Americans, my visceral reaction was that of ridicule and rejection. In my ignorance, the proposition sounded like another mass entitlement scheme and another impossible dream.

The reparations movement has grown from infancy to adolescence, and its body of literature has increased. Randall Robinson's recent book *The Debt: What America Owes Blacks*[1] is the manifesto of the genre to date. And universally high regard for the integrity and long-suffering of Atty. Robinson, in light of the significant role he played in freeing Nelson Mandela, dictates a reading of *The Debt*.

The Debt is a stream of consciousness which explains a plain negotiation — White Americans have, for centuries, benefited from unjust enrichment, gained by way of the barbarism their forefathers perpetrated against African-American slaves. Now the progeny of those slaves demand payment, demand their residuals of hope.

The American form of slavery was uniquely heinous and cruel. Lasting for 246 years (1619–1865), American slavery denied slaves any knowledge of or connection to their home region, culture, religion or customs; knowledge of their true family names; the right to earn their freedom; literacy; or legal status as a human being. American slave owners denied slaves wages for their work, let alone fair wages; bred people like cattle; killed people with impunity; mercilessly beat people; raped Black women or conscripted them to lives as concubines; killed or maimed people for trying to learn.

White Americans have appreciably benefited from the uncompensated ideas, inventions and labor of Black Americans and from the ongoing oppression and discouragement that their racist system created and perpetuated. In so doing, Whites provide their progeny with competitive advantages by way of inheritance.

Interest in Black reparations has been accelerated by the willingness of American and European governments to apologize to and compensate ethnic and religious groups for atrocities less diabolical than those experienced by Black slaves. The American government has apologized and paid reparations to the families of Japanese Americans who were detained for 5 years or fewer during World War II. Jewish families continue to receive reparations from Germany and Switzerland for the horrendous loss of life and the brutish expropriation of property experienced by Jews during the Holocaust. Six million Jews were slaughtered by the Germans. Estimates are that 150 million African/Americans were slain during slavery.

Although lengthy, a quote from *The Debt* is a classic. Robinson cites the book *Strong Men Keep Coming*[2] by Tonya Bolden, which includes a letter from a former slave master, Colonel P. H. Anderson.

Anderson had the audacity to write and ask one of his former slaves, Mr. Jourdon Anderson, to return from Dayton, Ohio, to Big Spring, Tennessee, to work for him again — this time as a free man. The following is the exquisite letter that ex-slave Jourdan Anderson wrote to his former slave master.

> Sir: I got your letter, and was glad to find that you had not forgotten Jourdon, and that you wanted me to come back and live with you again, promising to do better for me than anybody else can...
>
> I served you faithfully for thirty-two years, and Mandy twenty years. At twenty five dollars a month for me, and two dollars a week for Mandy, our earnings would amount to eleven thousand six hundred and eighty dollars. Add to this the interest for the time our wages have been kept back, and deduct what you paid for our clothing, and three doctor's visits to me, and pulling a tooth for Mandy, and the balance will show what we are in justice entitled to...
>
> If you fail to pay us for our faithful labors in the past, we can have little faith in your promises in the future. We trust the good Maker has opened your eyes to the wrongs which you and your fathers have done to me and my fathers, in making us toil for you for generations without recompense... Surely there will be a day of reckoning for those who defraud the laborer of his hire...[3]

Robinson states, as we could predict, that neither Col. Anderson nor Presidents Washington or Jefferson nor any of the slave masters have paid any of the tens of millions of slaves who, under threat of death, were required to work themselves to death to benefit generations of White people. Reparations have not been paid to any of the heirs of any of their slaves or former slaves.

Nonetheless, a doctoral dissertation could be written about the layers and implications of Mr. Jourdon Anderson's letter. For example, one of my beliefs is that slavery can be imposed on our bodies as well as our spirits. Slavery can be a mental condition. As such, slavery did not end in 1865. Rather, all of us, regardless of ethnicity, will be presented each day with multiple opportunities to choose to be a freed person or a slave. If we choose slavery, we can be slaves to our jobs, bosses, spouses, children, and habits. And like Col. Anderson, slavery will always give former slaves opportunities to return to old conditions and habits.

It is also clear that Mr. Jourdon Anderson was not only literate, he was articulate. Most importantly, Mr. Anderson was an early proponent of reparations. He established a monetary baseline for reparations — which can be used as a basis for calculating what is owed contemporarily.

Recently, I was emailed information on a website through which to research slave narratives.[4]

I was curious as to whether I could find the narratives of any of my relatives, so I entered the name "Odom" and received the narrative of Ms. Helen Odom and her mother Ms. Sarah Odom of Biscoe, Arkansas. Although the location does not match the location of my relatives, like Mr. Anderson's letter, I found the Odom narrative compelling.

Ms. Sarah Odom's grandmother Rachael (Ms. Helen Odom's great-grandmother) bore two children by her slave master, Temple. Temple never married but had three other children by another slave woman. When Temple died, he willed everything to his nearest relative, Jim McNeilly. Not only did none of Temple's resources go to support Temple's five Black children or their mothers, McNeilly added insult to injury by selling all of Temple's slaves for additional profit!

These slave women had to endure the indignity, brutality and forced labor of slavery, offering their bodies to the devil, and bearing his children more than once while his fortune was willed to enrich another devil who, instead of supporting his benefactor's children, multiplied the injustice by selling them. So, while Temple's money went elsewhere, the lifelong task of rearing his children fell to the most disenfranchised caste in America — Black slave women.

The evilness of the Temples and the Andersons against their slave women and their own Black children provides only glimpses of the 400 year long holocaust endured by Black Americans. Multiply the debt owed by Anderson and Temple to their slaves, times millions of slaves similarly situated and the total amount owed staggers the imagination.

The legacy of intergenerational poverty, disenfranchisement and dreams deferred has resulted in millions of Black Americans who survive rather than thrive. There are millions who exist without goals, plans, direction, or hope and whose only legacies are these same rotten outcomes.

While I benefited very much from reading *The Debt*, some specifics require development. Randall Robinson makes it clear that there is value in reparations reparteé. The question is, do Robinson and other leaders truly mean to achieve reparations? Does reparations represent a strategic goal, *a cause celebre*, a ploy or a conversation piece? The answer will determine how we are to proceed. Robinson says, "Even the *making* of a well-reasoned case for restitution will do wonders for the spirit of African Americans."[5] Further, he says that "[making] program recommendations...is not my strength. Nor is it the central point here. After all, we pretty much know what needs to be done. Blacks know this and whites know this."[6]

Obviously, *Saving Black America* disagrees with Robinson's assertion that White Americans either know or care about what needs to be done. Black people neither agree on what needs to be done or even how to do whatever might need to be done. If leaders and proponents are sincere and reparations truly is the long-term goal, then new economically based models for Black civil rights should serve as the backdrop for deliberations and plans.

Negotiate With Whom?

What would happen if, miracle of miracles, the federal government expressed its intent to discuss the possibility of paying reparations to Black people? That concession would beg the question, "Negotiate with whom?"

The worst case scenario is some version of the typical "Black panel of experts" featured at conferences and occasionally on television would be chosen to speak for us. These panels of experts tend to spend most of their time out-yelling, interrupting, contradicting, and upstaging each other. The best case scenario would be that a serious and internally aligned group of business-oriented Black Americans who are already busily engaged in pursuing economic development as a group-wide civil rights strategy would emerge to negotiate the deal.

The existence and work of a group like the National Board of Black Investment would make greater political progress in bringing about reparations discussions than would random rag-tag marches with eight hours of speakers full of sound and fury. In the freeing of Nelson Mandela, the equivalent of a responsible and representative group, the African National Congress, was primary. The existence of a serious organization comprised of competent like-minded representatives is the prerequisite to progress.

Considerations

Obviously, many profound issues must be addressed on the road to reparations. I will address a few of them in this section.

The Jim Crow Period

The reparations movement is based, as it should be, on the invidious, pervasive, and perennial heinousness of American slavery. It strains credulity, in our era of "instant gratification," to convince most people that a 135-year-old debt is still owed. Ours is an age that is molded by visual images. Adlai Stevenson once said, "The eyes of the world are on America." And a cynic later added, "And the eyes of America are on television."

If I see I'm more likely to believe, be it dogs and hoses turned on civil rights workers, soldiers returning in body bags, soldiers executing civilians, dead children being carried away from a bombed building, police officers mercilessly beating a man on the ground, Congressional hearings, a slow Bronco chase or vote recounts. See an image, believe.

The problem is, there are no moving pictures of slavery, and the photographs that were taken have the patina of incredulity. It has been said that our empathy for Holocaust survivors rests not so much on the accounts of victims, but more on the searing images in photographs and movies. Not only this, Jewish producers and directors have kept, as they should, the Holocaust alive in the consciousness of the world through succeeding generations of films, both fictional and documentary. There are also many museums, institutes, and foundations devoted to assuring that the Holocaust is neither forgotten nor repeated.

In this sense, the Jim Crow era is more important to the achievement of reparations than is slavery. There is no question that Jim Crow, which was the era of legal "separate but equal" laws, was slavery's aftershock, hiccuped from hell. There is no question that as odious as Jim Crow was, it could not compare to the devilishness of slavery. On the other hand, compared to the wrongs for which the world has been willing to pay reparations, the segregation era has currency. *De jure* segregation, which lasted from about 1877 until 1965 (or 88 years), followed *by de facto* segregation (from 1966 until the present) provide more than ample evidence for those so inclined to seek and pay reparations.

The lynchings, murders, bombings, maimings, beatings, intimidation, rape, disenfranchisement, theft of property, red lining, misappropriation of funds, fraud, false arrests and imprisonment, psychological torture, malfeasance, mischief, stress, undue hardships, damage to health and longevity, lies, discouragement, denial of equal protection and opportunities, denial of birthright and inheritance, inadequate representation, racist theories, miseducation, exclusion from membership and participation, slander, defamation, harassment, hostile environments, and humiliation created and imposed by legal separation are reasons enough for reparations, slavery notwithstanding.

We have Rosewood, Springfield and Black Tulsa, where the citizens of economically successful Black townships were massacred and the models of a Black economy were destroyed and successful Black cities forever discouraged. We have government sponsored murder of Black soldiers. We have court cases and legal precedents.

Moreover, we have pictures! Some in color! We have still photos, we have movies, both fictional and documentary. An excellent example is the horrific yet compelling "Without Sanctuary: Lynching Photography in America."[7] Without Sanctuary is a collection of photographs of Black men and women who were lynched, sometimes in groups. It chronicles a fraction of America's debt to Black America — how thousands of God-fearing, Bible-thumping murderous, complicit White people in the twentieth century took grinning pictures next to hanging, burning corpses. How many such people had picnics around lynched bodies and had the audacity to make and buy postcards of the carnage and send those cards around the country as greetings to loved ones. It would not take professors of philosophy to extrapolate from this evidence of the "separate-but-equal" era to imply what slavery may have been like.

Better still, we have live witnesses and victims. And unlike Holocaust and internment survivors, millions of our victims are still in their 40's!

And we have currency. Black Americans are the only ones whose right to vote comes before the U. S. Congress for a vote. The 1965 Voting Rights Act must again be ratified by the Congress in 2007. The NAACP, the Urban League, the Rainbow Coalition and other groups are in constant and protracted battles to redress wrongs in law and practice in every American sector. And hate groups in America and on the Internet are growing both in number and viciousness.

Basing reparations on Jim Crow is strategically superior to that of attempting to remind America of the erstwhile horrors of slavery.

Once and For All

Those who are seriously seeking reparations must be prepared to make them a "once and for all" deal. There is little reason to engage in reparations negotiations for symbolic purposes, especially if the only result is the transfer of billions of dollars to Black hands. The central reason to seek such negotiations should be to achieve a satisfactory conclusion — one sufficient enough to effect payment of the debt and to end the attendant acrimony. The results of reparations negotiations should be to *pay the debt*, thereby freeing America of the guilt and charges of slavery-based and Jim Crow-based racism. Reparations should represent payment in full. The agreed upon payment may be pennies on the dollar, but we are talking a lot of dollars and a lot of pennies.

If a reparations settlement does not result in a dramatic reduction of charges of racism, prejudice, discrimination, or victimization, there is little incentive for White Americans to agree to negotiate in good faith (if they ever will anyway). Reparations should result in a sea-change for Black Americans. They should result in a wholesale turning away from protests and a turning toward economic development of the sort *Saving Black America* espouses. If the payment of reparations does nothing to reduce the number of race-based complaints, lawsuits, demonstrations, and the general contentiousness, there is little reason to engage in reparations discussions.

Quid Pro Quo

Black idioms are elegant in their imagery and simplicity. One such idiom applies here: "You got to bring something to get something!" A corollary is, "You're too light behind! (You're not big enough to fight me!)" You have to bring some chips to the poker table. The higher the stakes, the more chips you have to bring. Got to bring something to get something. As a fisherman, it's generally true that the larger the bait, the larger the fish. Few fish species will attack bait that's larger than they are.

The point is that Black Americans have been more than mere victims of racism over the past century. The civil rights movement has resulted in significant gains and the construction of substantial organizational anti-racist armamentaria, especially since 1964.

Affirmative Action is a case in point. As a former Affirmative Action officer and supporter of Affirmative Action, I acknowledge that Affirmative Action has been good for Black Americans and that it has helped many more White people than it has ever helped us (White women, people with disabilities, people over 40, small business owners, etc.). Yet, Black people are recruited to defend Affirmative Action, and Black people are blamed for its shortcomings (or Whites' perception of its shortcomings).

For all the good that Affirmative Action has done, it may be time to view it like a good old family car that one trades in for a newer, better model. Affirmative Action maybe the something we bring to get something better. It would be a boon not to have to explain to one more bigot or ignoramus the difference between a quota and a goal. You pay substantial reparations and we support the dismantling of Affirmative Action programs. Besides, if reparations are decent, preferences and set-aside programs will be unnecessary.

The Willie Fulgear Syndrome

Yes, Willie Fulgear! Who is he and why is he relevant to this discussion? Prepare for an "Aha!" moment. A couple of years ago, when 52 academy awards were "misplaced," it was Black salvage man Willie

Fulgear who found and turned them in. The good news was that Mr. Fulgear was an instant hero and was rewarded $50,000for his honesty.

Later came the bad news. While on vacation, thieves broke into Mr. Fulgear's home and walked away with $40,000 in cash. $40,000 in cash in his home! Within a few months, Willie Fulgear went from poverty, to hero, to franchise, to poverty to an object of pity.

If my implied point remains unclear, let me make it plain. Brother Fulgear represents what happens to individuals who are unprepared to manage money. He represents professional ballplayers, lottery winners, and beneficiaries who go from abject poverty to wealth without the inclination, values, habits, education, or means to manage significant amounts of money, and who, unceremoniously, return to abject poverty. Willie Fulgear lives in tens of millions of Americans who lack the experience, education, or discipline to transcend a *carpe diem* (live for today), "easy-come-easy-go" philosophy about money.

More recently, there was the sad story of a Detroit woman whose home, built by Habitat for Humanity, was repossessed because she had stopped making mortgage payments. When asked about it, the woman said that she had been calling "those people" to come and fix her furnace, but "they" never came.

Similar to Brother Fulgear, this sister wasn't ready, in her case for home ownership. Short of buying a house outright, or better yet, inheriting one, a brand new low-interest Habitat home is one the best deals a low-income person can get. Habitat provides great housing, lots of equity and a solid economic base.

But somehow, along the way, this sister failed to be impressed by the difference between renting and owning. For home owners, there are no "those people" to come and fix anything, except for items under warranty, and even then responsibility is on the owner to make arrangements with repair persons. And, more importantly for owners, there is no connection between repairs and mortgage notes. This woman lost her best chance at middle class status simply because she lacked basic readiness for the next economic level.

Back to reparations, let's suppose that the leaders of the American government are inexplicably struck with remorse and are compelled to allocate $100 billion, or five percent, of America's current $2 trillion surplus to Black Americans as reparations-in-full. That would put in the hands of each of America's 35 million Black Americans approximately $28,000.

In the absence of an economic structure similar to the National Board of Black Investment as described in this book, the defining question is this: How long would it take for the majority of that $100 billion to be back in the hands of White Americans? In light of the experiences of Brother Fulgear and the sister from Detroit, what long-term good would $28,000 do for the average Black American? Will we be like beggars sitting on sacks of gold?

Preparations for reparations may be more important than reparations themselves. Preparations for reparations will encourage and support responsible management of personal resources so that if reparations never occur the majority of Black Americans will be more secure as a result of sound money management practices. If reparations ever occur, and they are more likely to occur for a money-wise *organized* constituency, Black Americans will be more likely to invest reparations to break the cycle of intergen-erational poverty, rather than squandering the blood-bought inheritance of our fore parents. Preparations for reparations should begin post haste.

> *We won't be going in there alone... I mean my ancestors. I will call into the past, far back to the beginning of time and beg them to come and help me at the judgment.*
>
> *I will reach back and draw them into me and they must come. For at this moment I am the whole reason they have existed at all.*
>
> —Lines by the character Cinque from the movie "Amistad"

CHAPTER 28

Only the Best Will Do

Planning without planning for change is planning for nothing but trouble.

It is critical that Black Americans take advantage of this time, in which no viable economic structure exists for us. The absence of a structure creates a void in our community. Without strategic planning, the void will be filled with a poor structure, which will, at best, produce confusion. Four examples support this thesis:

1. Immediately after the abolition of slavery, the victors assumed that the hole created in the social fabric of the South would be filled by the structure of freedom — life, liberty, and the pursuit of happiness for freed slaves. Admittedly, the Reconstruction era did replace slavery for a significant amount of time, but the length and damage of the Jim Crow period dwarfed the positive impacts and duration of the Reconstruction era.

2. Immediately after the Supreme Court handed down its decision in *Brown v. Topeka Board of Education*, it was assumed that school segregation was ended for all time. However, not only was *de jure* desegregation not eliminated in the ensuing 40 years, a replacement system of *de facto* segregation thrived. The long-standing structure of segregation was not replaced with a structure designed to ensure integration or educational equity.

3. Immediately after the signing of the 1964 Civil Rights Act, it was assumed that the systems of hatred and discrimination at work in

the areas of housing, public accommodations, transportation, etc., would end. It was also assumed that the War on Poverty would significantly reduce, if not eliminate, poverty in America. In the interim, few efforts have been made to replace old structures of discrimination with new structures designed to enhance life, liberty, and pursuits of happiness. Instead, civil rights structures exist only to fight old, oppressive structures.

4. Immediately after the fall of the Soviet Union, it was assumed that democracy would replace Communism. The void created by the fall of Communism was not filled with a structure designed to produce democracy, because no one thought of or planned such a design prior to the fall.

As the citizens of Russia now know for sure, the collapse of a system that oppresses a people does not mean that liberation automatically comes into being. As one pundit recently explained creation: Believing in evolution is the same as believing that a hurricane could blow through a junkyard and produce a 747 jet.

The plight of Black Americans persists not because we have been unsuccessful in fighting racism. It persists because the civil rights structure was designed to fight, to protest against, and bring down the structure of racism. We need to know racism's opposite. What do we call the state of being in which racism does not exist? It is difficult to work toward a vision no one has seen!

Getting rid of the old oppressive system creates a vacuum. Vacuums are not oppressive, but they can't save anyone. Building 747 jets — or civil rights strategies that produce life, liberty, and opportunities for happiness — result from proactive, positive plans and activities, not from nothing.

As I said earlier, Dr. King, in his most famous speech, used the partitive article "a," not the definite article "the." It was "I have *a* dream," not "I have *the* dream." That apparently minor but important linguistic difference empowered me to dream of this book and this model. With Dr. King's guidance, I shared *a* model, not *the* model.

If you don't like this model, or feel you can do better, good! I look forward to reading your model and to helping to make it a reality.

What are you waiting for? With all you say you want, there is:

A dream for you to follow:
A goal for you to set;
A plan for you to make;
A project for you to begin;

Only the Best Will Do

An idea for you to act on;
A possibility for you to explore;
An opportunity for you to grab;
A choice for you to make.

If not, you shouldn't have anything to talk about.[1]

—Iyanla Vanzant

CHAPTER 29

Dionte Revisited

"I'm feeling good from my head to my shoes,
Know where I'm going and I know what to do,
I've tidied up my point of view, I've got a new
    attitude!...
I'm changed for good..."

—Bunny Hill, Jon Gilutin,
Sharon T. Robinson
Recorded by Patti LaBelle

This book began with a tale of a boy named Dionte and the deplorable conditions of his life. Readers familiar with the lives of poor Black Americans know children like Dionte and children worse off. Dionte was never abandoned, nor was he physically or sexually abused. Unfortunately, we have to be grateful for that which we should be able to take for granted.

Given this vision of an economically-based civil rights model, it would be reasonable to ask how Dionte's life might be impacted. Visions of the impact on Dionte's life can be seen from one of two perspectives. "What would Dionte's life be like had he been born after the full implementation of the economic model?" or "How would Dionte's life change were the economic model implemented during his childhood?"

The second perspective would require a discussion of a transition period. Transition periods are characteristically fraught with chaos, and they frequently last for many years. Also, cutting and leading edge individuals are the first to capitalize on any societal change. As a result, were an economic model implemented immediately, it is likely that years would pass before Dionte's mother would become aware of the change and would learn how to take full advantage of changes, such as learning job skills, deciding to become an entrepreneur, learning to develop a business plan, qualifying for a home mortgage, etc.

So, for the sake of brevity, I choose to envision Dionte being born after the full implementation of an economic model. This view facilitates brevity because, but for a few cultural nuances, Black children should lead a Black version of the lives led by average American children. The profoundly average life of a White child in America marks a profound improvement for the average Black child. So, let us make note that what is ordinary for White children and is, at the same time, quite extraordinary for Black ones.

In a new, economically based era, Dionte will:

- be conceived by a loving, married couple;

- receive high quality pre-natal care;

- be carried to term by a healthy, happy mother;

- be born healthy, of average size and weight;

- receive quality pediatric care;

- have adequate health insurance;

- know that his parents and family love him;

- have a baby sister, Chaniqua;

- live in a family in which his parents are middle class;

- live in a family in which parents are gainfully employed;

- live in a safe neighborhood;

- attend high quality schools which will challenge him academically;

- perform as an "average" to "above average" student;

- learn about American History, Black History, and business;

- graduate from high school;

- attend and graduate from a post-secondary educational institution paid for by family savings;

- have no negative interaction with the criminal justice system;

- become gainfully employed;

- continue his education;

- contribute attention and time to helping the youth of his community;

- practice religion;

- marry, have children, rear and care for them;

- start and grow a business;

- receive an inheritance from a relative;

- do business with other Black Americans as often as possible;

- live a long, healthy life;

- leave a personal legacy and

- leave a substantial estate to his heirs and the National Board of Black Investment

At a minimum, Dionte, Shantel, and Chaniqua deserve average and ordinary. Exceptional and extraordinary contributions are facilitated from such a platform.

CHAPTER 30

Go, Buy For Yourselves

Sermon written and delivered by the author's late father, to a group of students in 1954, after the Brown v. Board of Education Supreme Court decision.

Rev. Corey Franklin Odom, Sr.
(1908-1979)

"But the wise answered, saying, Not so; lest there be not enough for us and you: but go ye rather to them that sell, and buy for yourselves."

—Matthew 25:9

There is no country in the entire world that affords the human race better opportunities for the creation and possession of utilities than does America. Despite the fact that there are limitations placed upon our once enslaved group, all are at liberty to produce and possess more. All things being equal, there is no excuse for one individual to sit by the wayside and beg others. It is at once conceded that length of time has much to do with one's chances to accumulate more than one whose time to accumulate has been much shorter, however, one is judged not by the length of time one has had, but by one's ability and one's opportunity to use the time at one's disposal.

Despite the fact that our previous condition of servitude has relegated us to the rear...; despite the fact that we have been and remain maltreated in many instances and places; despite the fact that we are treated with less respect than the brute on many occasions; and despite the fact that our treatment is uncivil in many places; no insurmountable barrier is placed in our path to produce and possess utilities.

The plea "Give us of your oil" most often comes from those of our group who engage in predatory activities — who become the very personification of the foolish virgins, who, when their lamps were going out, to keep from being in total darkness, assumed the roles of mortified mendicants, pleading "Give us of your oil."

By oil, I mean sustenance for the human family, resources for survival and growth. Every well organized group in our country has had time enough and money enough to purchase oil. The foolish virgins had oil enough for the present, had the bridegroom come when they expected him, but the seeming delay of the bridegroom's coming, and the short-sightedness on the part of the foolish virgins placed them in a beggar's position.

Not knowing what the future will bring forth, it is incumbent upon us to make ample preparation. To go to sleep, to follow others — not having made themselves secure with the necessary commodity — was calamitous, and earned for the five virgins the label "foolish."

Demands for our commodity will decrease our supply. There would have been much ground for criticism had the foolish virgins no money with which to buy, or had there been no oil for sale, or had the salesman refused to give service, but the foolish virgins had the money, the store was open for business, and the salesman would have been glad to sell. "Not so," said the wise, for you had the same chance as we. "Not so," said the wise, "for there was no good reason why you should have slept, when you knew your supply was low."

Our race, it is true, is young on these shores, and far too young to keep company with many of the things that are destroying us. We are too young to own more cars than homes, more honky-tonks than decent business establishments. We are too young to have more teenage girls serving as barmaids than learning as students. We are too young to spend more money on strong drinks and worldly pleasures than we do on education.

Travel this country over and your ears will be deafened with cries coming from our group bemoaning their condition. Their cry to the South, "Give us of your oil," their cry to the North that once listened,

"Give us of your oil," but from every direction comes the answer now, "Not so, go buy for yourselves"...

The world is watching our bank accounts; the eyes of the races are upon us as we have come into possession of more than 15,948,512 acres of land, and buildings valued at more than $1.5 billion. The world is taking due notice as we organize, for we have a National Business League, the National Negro Bankers' Association, the National Association of Funeral Directors, the National Negro Insurance Association, Negro fraternal organizations; the National Negro Retail Merchant Association. We are doing an annual business of billions of dollars. Negroes have bought towns and paid cash for them. The world is taking notice as the Negro is becoming integrated into labor unions. Some of us get as much per day as anyone else, wear the best clothes, live in comfortable homes, and eat the best food. We've gone from driving an oxcart to a $28,000 Dusenberg car.

Yet we beg, "Give us of your oil." No wonder other groups are telling us, "Not so. With the progress you have made, do for yourselves." As individuals, we do fairly well, but as a group, we are to be pitied.

We ought to stop complaining until we get our heads, senses, and pocketbooks together. Put up some decent places for ourselves so our girls and women will not have to run from Dan to Beersheba to be insulted. We cannot say that we do not have the money, because we do. We throw away enough money in every community every month to put up a thriving business. We are just foolish like those virgins were — sleeping, to wake up too late.

Someone will raise the question, "Why build businesses?" Why do any of these progressive things? We are striving for integration. Well and good, but...in a recent meeting of our church, we were discussing ways and means to endow our five colleges. One brother raised the question, "With the Supreme Court decision of May 17th last, why bother?" Bishop (B. Julian) Smith answered, "We need to take some fine schools into integration as well as become beneficiaries of other fine schools." That's the answer.

There is another side to this thing, we must turn out boys and girls with business sense. We have dying businesses all over the country. Half of the business managers do not have any business sense. They get rich too quickly, too independently... They permit a crowd of ruffians to hang around, their prices are above everybody else's. They want to get rich in a month.

If the cry was made now that our group will not be sold this thing nor served at that place, we will stand speechless — like the mummies, sphinxes and obelisks of Egypt.

The herald has already sounded the alarm for us — "go and buy for ourselves." If we buy for ourselves and from ourselves, it will make more jobs for ourselves, and we can better help ourselves. We spend thousands of dollars each year with a certain insurance company, perhaps, one of the largest in the world, and the best prepared in our group cannot even be the janitor of the building. If you ask for a job, the singing sarcastic voice is heard "Not so, go do business for yourselves."

Myers, in his general history says "The Negro will always be a hewer of wood and a drawer of water for his more fortunate brother." Rightly so, if we continue to dump our money where it will not be seen again. Our wells are full of water, our forests are dense with timber. Let us draw and hew for ourselves. Our social status is based on our economic status.

When our economic independence will let us point to smoke stacks of factories, when our economic independence will let us deafen the ears of the world with revolving wheels and flying shuttles of industrial plants; when our economic independence will let us darken human eyes with greenbacks and flying eagles; then and only then, will our group get its proper recognition. The world will beat a path to the door of any individual of our group whose sign reads "Economically Independent" or "Economically Comfortable."

Because of our foolish actions, our lamps are going out.

(1) The lamp of employment for all too many of us is almost out. In all too many instances we are not pushed out of employment because of our color, but because of little things — Blue Mondays and Red Tuesdays, an excursion, a little bad feeling, and other trivial matters...

"Go, and buy for yourselves" — these are not the words of Bye and Seager, in *Principles of Economy*, nor the sayings of Cassel, in his theory of *Social Economy*, nor Taylor, nor even Carver in *Social Justice*, nor Clay or Tawney on *The Acquisitive Society*. They are the words of the greatest economist and teacher this world has ever known, Jesus Christ, who promoted individual action and self-assertion.

He meant "go and do things for yourselves," when he told the blind man to go to Siloam's Pool and wash. He meant "go and do things for yourselves" when He ordered the man with the withered hand "To stretch it forth"; and when He commanded the inactive man, who had lain thirty eight years on the porch of Bethesda to take up his bed and walk. Jesus would have the individual or group, or the race, realize that salvation is from within.

(2) Our lamp of racial integrity is almost out. There is no race in all the world that has a richer and more enviable heritage and background than the Negro race; the Muse of history, who dips his quill into

170

the meteoric flash of absolute erudition, will attest to the fact that we are identified with the world's greatest civilization. There flows through our veins some of the best blood... Despite this fact, my people go through this world obsessed with an inferiority complex, which has forged chains to bind the race more tightly than the chains of slavery.

The mimicry or imitation of the race is deplorable. To be more practical, we are trying to be more like the other racial group, trying to get away from ourselves. To my way of thinking, each race is to make a definite contribution to complete the world. Our contribution is that others learn from us the expression of deep spiritual truths. We call it emotionalism. A White minister said that his church needed "re-emotionalizing" because it is too cold.

Our folks are trying to become like them. There was a time when the White man sang, "Give me the whole world, and the Negro can have Jesus." But Jesus has done so much for the Negro that he is now singing, "Give me Jesus," too. Now the Negro picks up the song the White man once sang, "Give me the whole world and the White man can have Jesus."...

What both groups need to do is "Seek ye first the kingdom of God and His righteousness, and all these things will be added..."

We are trying to change our color and become white and red. Red lips, red cheeks, red fingernails, red toenails. And while we are trying to turn white and red, the other race is trying to become tan. The pigmentation, the hue of our skin is no great barrier to us...

If you are able to buy oil for yourselves and will act like the wise virgins, no man can keep you away from the wedding feast. The world is not averse to our having this and that, enjoying this privilege and that privilege, but the world will not stand as our nurse any longer. Whatever is wanted "Go, buy for yourselves."

We need not lose our racial integrity or racial identity to secure recognition for ourselves, but we do need to lose [poor habits], such as being late, noisy, rough, tough, uncouth, disrespectful, and careless.

Finally, our spiritual lamps are going out. If there is any group that should go and buy the oil of grace for themselves, it is ours. In his book, *The Negro in the Methodist Church*, Crum says "Religion did two things for him: 1) It kept up his spirit in bondage, 2) It lessened the hand of the oppressor."

There is much yet that God wants to do for the Negro if he will let him. We should purpose in our hearts never to follow after strange gods. We should never become so intellectual that we should ever fail to look up to the hills from whence cometh our help. We need the oil of grace, that which will keep forever aglow the spark of religious life, the highest life and the best life, the life that is given in Christian service.

Go, now, dear fellow students, and purchase the oil of grace, for you cannot enter into life, that abundant life, without it.

If you will purchase this oil for yourselves, when time shall lose itself into eternity, and the onward march of progress will be halted by the traffic cops of the air; if you will purchase this oil for yourselves, when Aurora, with the golden tips of her fingers, shall open up the gray dawn of the morning, and the King of Day shall come forth out of his eastern bed, looking like a ball of fire, hurled from the stomach of liquid Vesuvius, driving down the amber-paved highway of the Levant — announcing the consummation of all things, you will join that religious scholastic group, to experience that which eye hath not seen, nor ear heard, nor man's heart conceived; things which God hath prepared for them that love Him.

Go, go, my race, buy oil for yourselves and from yourselves.

CHAPTER 31

Conclusions

I am delighted that you have chosen to take this mental and spiritual journey with me to a better place for Black Americans. As a teacher, I respect the differences in learning styles. There are those who prefer to draw their own conclusions from books, lectures and sermons. Those individuals may want to skip this chapter. If you do, I thank you for your attention thus far and trust that some of the contents of Saving Black America holds meaning, value and fruit for you.

To those who prefer that writers and speakers draw conclusions, I do so in the spirit of Emily Dickinson who said, "When pressed for rules and verities, all I know on earth are these..."

If pressed for conclusions, I proffer the following.

Pay greater attention to the unwritten and powerful model that direct Black attitudes and behaviors.

Realize that the current model did not always exist and, as a result, it can be changed.

Focus on the needs of our children, the negatives in the lives they are living and the possibilities for the positive lives than can live in a world where Black adults have our economic act together.

Act like a group. Have honest differences of opinions, but work for the betterment of our ethnic group.

Pay more attention to prevention.

Assume leadership responsibility.

Learn about the current (legislative-protest) model that came into existence and why it has prevailed.

See and be guided by a new, empowering vision for Black America.

Learn from the successful economic models of other groups.

Establish criteria for a new economically based model.

Develop a framework for a new economically based model.

Develop a new model for Black civil rights and consider the Odom model.

Apply the new models to problems that vex Black Americans.

Identify and overcome mental barriers to Black success.

Plan the kick-off celebration, the jubilee.

Assist all Black Americans to make preparations for reparations whether or not reparations occur.

Develop the best plans we can.

Adhere to the Biblical admonition to take care of ourselves.

Readers who are interested in contacting me about *Saving Black America*, please do so at www.odom@chorus.net.

APPENDIX

WHY I'M STILL BLACK

"Suppose we arose tomorrow morning and lo! instead of being "Negroes," all the world called us "Cheiropolidi" — do you really think this would make a vast and momentous difference to you and to me? Would you be any less ashamed of being descended from a black man or would your school-mates feel any less superior to you? The feeling of inferiority is in you, not in any name. The name merely evokes what is already there. Exorcise the hateful complex and no name can ever make you hang your head."[1]

—W. E. B. DuBois

"What's my name?"[2]

—Muhammad Ali

"Hush, hush, somebody's calling my name. Oh my Lord, oh my Lord, what shall I do?"

—Negro Spiritual

I am still "Black" and I refer to my people as "Black," not "African American." I do this deliberately. As a speaker on Black issues and diversity, my stubborn use of "Black" has been called dated and unenlightened by some colleagues of academe. But my preference for "Black" is not the result of my inability to learn or change. Rather, I hold that a people that can't agree on what they are to be called cannot agree on the solutions to the life and death challenges they face. In other words, the ability to agree on a name creates a decision-making pattern and precedent, a template, which will be very useful in the making of other key decisions.

175

The following 10 arguments influenced my continuous use of "Black."

Argument #1: We Chose "Black"

We chose to call ourselves Black. The psycholin-guistic power to change one's name is a symbol of freedom, but it can be taken to extremes. The progression of our names in this century has gone something like this: colored to Negro to Afro-American to Black to African American, with the ever-present nigger as an epithet through it all. Afro-American was the first name we chose for ourselves. However, we should resist the temptation to become "name happy!" At some point, the re-naming process should end, and "Black" should represent the end. That we cannot make up our minds for more than twenty years at a time is no compliment to our vision or our leadership.

Argument #2: We Need to Make Up Our Minds

Our social landscape is littered with names. Our institutions carry the residue of our indecisiveness. We still have such organizations as the National Association for the Advancement of *Colored* People, United *Negro* College Fund, *Afro-American* history departments, Congressional *Black* Caucus, and *African American* History Month.

While doing doctoral research at the University of Wisconsin in 1976, I became incensed when I discovered that information about Black people was listed in the card catalog under Negro. Proud and indignant, I called for the head librarian and proceeded to raise her consciousness about what we should be called. Her response was something like, "Sir, do you have any idea how many volumes we have in this library? How many cross-reference cards we have in our card catalog files? How often have Black people changed their name?" Her point was that since our name has changed so often, it would be a monumental task to update the card catalog system each time. I felt like Algonquin J. Calhoun, the jack leg lawyer in the Amos & Andy television series, after having been dressed down by a judge. Needless to say, I slinked back to my little desk, then slipped silently into the book stacks.

Argument #3: Multiple Names Confuse Others

Multiple names signal confusion. In my diversity and Affirmative Action training sessions, I am often asked, "What do we call your group?" My response is "Black or African American." These questions, for the most part, are not asked out of ignorance or insensitivity. Rather,

176

they reflect the fact that many Black Americans aren't sure. In order to communicate our expectations, we must first be able to communicate our name without hesitation.

Argument #4: African American Is Too Long

"African American" is a syntactic nightmare. It contains seven syllables, which can be very difficult to drag through paragraphs. For example, "We need more African American actors starring in more African American movies, directed by African American directors, owned by African American production companies." What we need is parsimony, simplicity, and elegance, i.e., "Black."

Argument #5: "African American" Is Inaccurate

"African American" will never achieve the accuracy to which it aspires. If P. W. Botha were to become an American citizen, he would be an African American. He is a citizen of South Africa. If the argument is that his people do not hail from Africa, then there is an argument that Black people do not hail from America.

This argument is more than theoretical. A while ago, a student from South Africa became a U. S. citizen and applied for admission to Georgetown University. On the application form, he appropriately checked the box "African American." After being admitted, it was discovered that the student was White. The university attempted to revoke the admission on the grounds that the student was admitted under false pretexts. The student's appeal was upheld based on the conclusion that he truly was African American.

While we're at it, this notion that being American and being a citizen of the United States are synonymous smacks of the same kind of narcissistic jingoism against which Black people rail. The United States is but one of many nations in the Americas. Therefore, are we Black African United Statesers?

Argument #6: The True Experts Aren't Using "African American"

The brothers and sisters on the street aren't referring to us as "African Americans." Listen to those who do use African American long enough and they will lapse into using Black. If the terms are synonymous, why change?

Argument #7: Everyone's in the Diaspora

I understand and empathize with the need to link the African Diaspora, yet, in a very real way, all humans are members of the African Diaspora, since human life began on the African continent and all continents were once part of the African continent.

We relinquish our claim as the founding members of the human family by limiting our Diaspora. We relinquish a genealogical and psychological advantage when we narrow our group focus. All Americans are African Americans, and all people belong to the African Diaspora whether or not they want to belong. Thereby, "African American" does not truly distinguish us from others.

Argument #8: Black Africans Don't View Us As African

A recent article addressed the issue of how Black Africans feel about visiting and repatriating African Americans. Many Africans are disdainful of the American assumption that distant biological ties necessarily mean kinship. The article quoted Africans who were both irked and amused at the "African American" assumption that upon touching African soil, we are home.

The study of sub-Saharan Africa — its nations, politics, geography, and differences — has not been a high priority for the majority of African Americans. As a result, relations between African Africans and Africans are neither normal or consistent. The social and political distance between African Americans and Black Africans has been widened due to general African American indifference to the needs and plight of Black Africans. A glaring example of this point was offered in a Black History Month feature done by reporter David Aldridge for ESPN's Sports Center, which aired on February 25, 1999. The piece featured (the Atlanta Hawks) stand-out center Dikembe Mutumbo. Mutumbo has dedicated his life to improving the lives of his countrymen in the Congo. Citizens of the Congo suffer needlessly from treatable and immunizable diseases, and people die for want of simple medical treatments.

Among many other humanitarian efforts, the multilingual Mutumbo, who came to America to study medicine, has personally pledged $2.5 million to build a hospital in the Congo. He has appealed to his multimillionaire African American professional basketball colleagues to support this $40 million Congo hospital project, but has received support from an embarrassingly small number of players, most of whom are fellow Georgetown alumni. Supporters include Patrick Ewing, Alonzo Mourning and Gary Peyton. Others include former coach John Thompson, and Wes Unsel. Several African American players have told Mutumbo that they would visit the Congo with him during summers, but none have followed through.

That our wealthiest young Black Americans refuse to make even a modest contribution to such a worthy cause is telling. However hellish and heinous our holocaust, unfortunately, bloodlines alone does not obviate four hundred years of absence from Africa. Black Americans must work hard to establish our credibility, authenticity and credentials with citizens of African nations. That Africans are as puzzled as White Americans at our singular claims to Africa emboldens me all the more to say that I am Black.

Argument #9: Black is a Higher Level of Being

I've always felt that Blackness was a status one achieved and something to strive for. "African American" is based on biology and geography, but Blackness is driven by spirit, emotion, psyche, and will ("Say it loud, I'm Black and I'm proud"). For example, it makes sense to say, "He's African American but he's not Black!" To say "He's Black but he's not African American" holds little meaning or weight. Although I know some White people who are culturally Black, I also know some African American people who are culturally White. I don't put them down. These are cultural choices people should be able to make — as long as they don't try to benefit from membership in two groups. I mean, they have to choose a side. African American people who are culturally White should not benefit from Affirmative Action or register as a disadvantaged business. Instead, they should "Pull themselves up by their own bootstraps!"

Every movement, every era, has its excesses and the Black power era was no exception, including militancy and "Blackploitation" films. Obviously, the excesses should be dropped by the next era, but we've lost some aspects of the era that should have been sustained across succeeding eras. In the Black Power movement, we called each other "brother" and "sister." We acknowledged each other's presence with special handshakes and head nods. We had a greater tendency to look out for one another. Time moves on, but our concern for one another need not.

The Black power era in America established and reinforced some positive norms in Black America that are lacking in the present era. There was a collective sense of pride, of brotherhood and sisterhood. We were family, community and group focused. We were concerned about equality, equity, and our image. People who insisted on embarrassing the group by their behaviors were called to account for themselves.

Gangsta rappers and guests on the *Jerry Springer* would have had to explain themselves.

I am Black and will remain so because I see no good reason to be someone else.

Argument #10: Let's Agree on Goals and Strategies

If Black academicians can agree on something, anything, let them agree on preventing Black-on-Black murders, improving our academic achievement, stopping the AIDS epidemic, caring for our elderly, and finding jobs for those who want to work. If our talented tenth can agree on anything, let renaming ourselves fall low on our collective "to do" list. If they can come to agreement on the critical issues, we can be called "blessed."

At this writing, language usage has borne out the position of we die-hards refused to change to "African American." Black is back — in recent books, articles, and music. And that's music to my ears.

BIBLIOGRAPHY

Introduction

1. Ryan, Michael. *"My Middle Name Is Persistence."* (New York Parade, October 8, 2000) p.24-25.

2. Barker, Joel Arthur. The Power of Vision: Discovering the Future Series. (Burnsville, MN: Charthouse, 1993)

3. Kettering, Charles F. *The Kettering Digest* (C.F. Kettering Foundation, 1956) p.4.

4. Machiavelli, Nicolo, The Prince, 1505.

5. *Best Loved poems of the American People.* (New York: Doubleday, 1936) p.102.

6. Odom, Corey F. Sr. *"Go Buy for Yourselves."* (unpublished, 1954).

7. Hyams, Joe. *Zen in the Martial Arts* (New York: Bantam Books 1982).

8. Odom, Corey F. Sr. *"A Long Patience."65* (unpublished)

Chapter 1: Dionte

1. Neenan, Julia McNamee. *"Having No Dad Affects Black Boys' Self-Esteem."* The Men's Health Network. www.healthscout.com/cgi-bin/Web-Objects/Af?ap=197&id=102725. September 18, 2000. p.2.

2. Joint Center for Political and Economic Studies. "Birth Rates and Infant Mortality." www.jointcenter: org/databank/factsht/infanth.html. June 1999. p.2.

3. U.S. National Center for Health Statistics Reports, vol. 47, no. 25, *"Life Expectancy at Birth By Race and Sex, 1940-1998."* www.cdc.gov/nchs. October 5, 1999.

4. The Journal of Blacks in Higher Education. *"The Two Nations of Black America."* www.pbs.org/wgbh/pages/frontline/shows/race/economics/vital.html. Summer and Winter, 1997.

5. Joint Center for Political and Economic Studies, p.1.

6. Miller, Jerome G. *Search and Destroy: African American Males in the Criminal Justice System.* (Cambridge University Press, 1996), p.6.

7. Mann, Taynia *"Profile of African Americans, 1970-1995."* The Black Collegian Online, 1997.

8. El Nasser, Haya. *"Census Shows Greater Numbers of Hispanics."* USA Today, March 8, 2001, p.3A.

9. Joiner, Lottie L., *"The State of Black Children."* Emerge, October, 1998. p.39.

10. Americans for Divorce Reform. *"Divorce Statistics: Effects on Black Community."* www.divorcereform.org/black.html

11. Griffin, Regina, *"Black Women and Breast Cancer."* http://www. findarticles.com/m1321/1998_Oct_24/53177327/pl/article.jhtml

12. Reuters Health. *"Heart Disease Toll Heavier on Blacks, Southern-ers.",* June 21, 2001.

13. Melville, Nancy A. *"Video Addresses Black Men, Prostate Cancer."* Health Scout, 2000.

14. Washington, Harriet A. *"Vital Signs: An Unhealthy Year for Blacks."* Emerge. December/January, 1999.

15. Reuters Health. *"Blacks Missing Out on Quality Asthma Care: Study.",* July 9, 2001.

16. Associated Press. *"CDC See Racial Gap in Flu Shots."* June 28, 2001. www.nlm.nih.gov/medlineplus/news/fullstory_2458.html

17. Centers for Disease Control and Prevention. *"HIV & AIDS Trends."* September 9, 1998.

18. Centers for Disease Control and Prevention.

19. Stolberg, Sheryl Gay. *"Eyes Shut, Black America is Being Ravaged By AIDS."* The New York Times National, June 29, 1998). A1.

Bibliography

20. Joiner, 39.

21. Joiner, 39.

22. Lusane, Clarence, *"Plenty of Blame to Go Around for Blacks Inaction on AIDS."* October, 1998.

23. Washington.

24. Stolberg.

25. Beck, Joan. *Object of Undesire* (Chicago Tribune, October 19, 1998) Section 1, p.21.

26. Elias, Marilyn *"Racism and High Blood Pressure."* USA Today, October 24, 1996, 3D.

27. U.S. Department of Justice, *"Prisoners in 1996."* June 11, 1997, p.9.

28. U.S. Statistical Abstract 2000.

29. Frontline, p.2.

30. Frontline.

31. Miller, p.6.

32. Miller, p.7.

33. Miller, p.54.

34. Miller, p.107.

35. Alford, Harry C. *"The State of Black Business,"* The Madison Times, July 1, 1998.

36. Alford.

37. Stephens, Brooke. *Talking Dollars and Making Sense: A Wealth Building Guide for African Americans*. (New York: McGraw-Hill, 1997).

38. Reuters. "U.S. Poverty Lowest Since 1979, Income Record High." September 30, 1999.

39. Reuters. September 30, 1999.

40. *"Blacks Own Three Percent of Nation's Businesses"* JET Magazine (July 20, 1992) p.46.

41. U.S. Department of Commerce, Bureau of the Census. *"Poverty in the United States,"* 1998.

42. Frontline, p.2.

43. Frontline, p.4.

44. Bracey, Gerald, Phi Delta Kappan, November, 1998.

45. Rifkin, Jeremy, *The End of Work: The Decline of the Global Labor Force and the Dawn of the Post Market Era* (New York: G.P. Putnam & Sons, 1995).

46. Rifkin, 69.

47. Rifkin, 79.

48. Rifkin, 79.

49. Rifkin, 80.

50. Schorr. Lisbeth B., *Within Our Reach: Breaking the Cycle of Disadvantage.* (New York: Doubleday, 1988).

Chapter 3: The "Where Do We Go From Here?" Question

1. Kimbro, Dennis and Hill, Napoleon. *Think and Grow Rich: A Black Choice.* (New York: Falcon Crest, 1991).

2. Stephens.

3. Fraser, George C. *Race for Success: The Ten Best Business Opportunities For Blacks In America.* (New York: William Morrow, 1998).

4. Weems, Robert E. Jr. *Desegregating the Dollar: African American Consumerism in the Twentieth Century.* (New York: NY University Press, 1998).

Bibliography

5. Woodson, Robert L., Editor. *On The Road To Economic* Freedom: An Agenda For Black Progress. (Washington D.C.: Regnery Gateway, 1987).

6. Orman, Suze. *The 9 Steps To Financial Freedom: Practical and Spiritual Steps So You Can Stop Worrying.* (New York: Crown Publishers, 1997.)

7. Oprah, Harpo Productions, January 18, 1999.

8. Oprah.

9. Oprah.

10. Remarks by the President in ESPN Live: *A Conversation with the President, Sports and Race: "Running In Place?"* (The White House Office of the Press Secretary, April 14, 1998).

11. ESPN.

12. ESPN.

13. National Bar Association. *Civil Rights and the Supreme Court* (C-Span Archives, July 29, 1998).

Chapter 4: Leadership Responsibility

1. Fraser, 281.

2. Fraser, 281.

3. Fraser, 281.

4. Stephens.

5. Stephens, 16.

6. Steele, Shelby. *The Content of Our Character: A New Vision of Race In America.* (New York: HarperPerennial, 1991).
7. Steele, 16.

8. Woodson.

9. Woodson, 23.

10. Fraser, 6.

11. Fraser, 84.

12. Fraser, 58.

13. Berry, Mary Frances. *"Color Codes: Moving Beyond Clinton's Race Initiative Means Facing A Black White Reality and Building Bridges."* (Emerge: December/January, 1999) p.60.

14. West, Cornell. *Race Matters.* (Boston: Beacon Press, 1993) pp.6-7.

15. Weems, Robert E. Jr. *Desegregating the Dollar: African American Consumerism in the Twentieth Century.* (New York: NY University Press, 1998).

16. Weems, 131.

17. Miller, Jerome G. *Search and Destroy: African American Males in the Criminal Justice System.* (Cambridge UK: Cambridge Univ. Press, 1996) p.107.

18. Miller, xii.

19. Berry, 58.

Chapter 6: The History of the Current Model

1. McNeil, Genna Rae. *Groundwork: Charles Hamilton Houston and The Struggle For Civil Rights.* (Philadelphia: University of Pennsylvania Press, 1983).

2. McNeil, 3.

Chapter 7: The Current Model

1. Odom, John Yancy. *Educational Administration and Human Relations: An Integration.* (Madison: University of Wisconsin, 1978) p.219.

2. Terry, Robert W. *FOR WHITES ONLY.* (Grand Rapids: William B. Eerdmans, 1970).

Chapter 8: I Have A Dream II

1. King, Martin Luther Jr. *Speech at The Civil Rights March on Washington.* (August 28, 1963.)

Chapter 9: American Jewish Federations

1. Miller, Charles. *An Introduction To The Jewish Federation.* (New York: Council of Jewish Federations, 1985) p.6.

2. Miller, 3.

3. Miller, 9.

4. Miller, 5.

5. Miller, 6.

6. Miller, 6.

7. Miller, 7.

8. Miller, 7.

Chapter 10: The "Caisses Populaires" of Quebec, Canada

1. Caron, Rene and Poire, Marin. *The Unbelievable Power of Cooperation.* (September 18, 1990).

2. Caron and Poire.

3. Caron and Poire.

Chapter 12: A Framework for a New Model

1. Goodson, Max. (Discussions with, 1973)

Chapter 13: A New Model For Black Civil Rights

1. Taylor, Mildred D. *Roll of Thunder, Hear My Cry.* (New York: Bantam Books, 1978).

2. Heron, Gil Scott. *"Willing"* (from the Album "Willing" New York, Arista Records, 1980).

3. Hornsby, Bruce. *"The Way It Is"* (from the Album "The Way It Is": New York: RCA, 1986).

Chapter 15: Education

1. Mayer, Martin, extemporaneous comments made at the Institute for the Development of Educational Activities Conference of the Kettering Foundation, Atlanta Georgia, 1978.

2. McNeil, 134.

3. McNeil, 134.

4. Lester, Julius. *Look Out Whitey! Black Power's Gon' Get Your Mama.* (New York: Grove Press, 1968) p.30.

Chapter 17: The Criminal (In)Justice System

1. Miller.

2. Cole, David. No *Equal Justice: Race and Class in American Criminal Justice System* (New York: The New Press, 1999).

3. Schlosser, Eric. *"The Prison Industrial Complex."* (The Atlantic Monthly, December, 1998) pp. 51-77.

Chapter 22: Barrier Three: Raising Hell for the Hell of It

1. "The Road To Brown", videotape PBS version, California Newsreel, San Francisco.

Bibliography

Chapter 23: Barrier Four: Too Many Words

1. deHuszar, George B. *Practical Applications of Democracy*. (New York: Harper and Brothers, 1945).

2. Hayakawa, S.I. *Language in Thought and Actions*. (Chicago: Harcourt Brace Jovanovich, 1972).

Chapter 27: Preparations for Reparations

1. Robinson, Randall. *The Debt: What America Owes to Blacks*. (New York: Putton, 2000).

2. Bolden, Tonya. *Strong Men Keep Coming*. (New York: John Wiley & Sons, 1999).

3. Bolden.

4. Born in Slavery: Slave Narratives from the Federal Writers' Project, 1936-1938, 30410. pp.226-227.

5. Robinson, p.232.

6. Robinson, p.238.

7. Allen, James, et al. Without Sanctuary: Lynching Photography in America. (Twin Palms Publishers: 2000).

Chapter 31: Go, Buy for Yourselves

1. Odom, Corey F., Sr.

NOTES

NOTES

NOTES

NOTES

NOTES

NOTES